PENGUIN BOOKS

TRAIL OF HAVOC

Patrick Marnham was a reporter for *Private Eye* and also worked as the literary editor of *The Spectator*. His books include *Road to Katmandu, Fantastic Invasion: Dispatches from Africa*, and *So Far from God: A Journey to Central America*, which won the Thomas Cook Travel Award, 1985. He lives in Paris.

PATRICK MARNHAM

Trail of Havoc

PENGUIN BOOKS

PENGUIN BOOKS
Published by the Penguin Group
Viking Penguin, a division of Penguin Books USA Inc.
40 West 23rd Street, New York, New York 10010, U.S.A.
Penguin Books Ltd, 27 Wrights Lane, London W8 5TZ, England
Penguin Books Australia Ltd, Ringwood, Victoria, Australia
Penguin Books Canada Ltd, 2801 John Street,
Markham, Ontario, Canada L3R 1B4
Penguin Books (N.Z.) Ltd, 182-190 Wairau Road,
Auckland 10, New Zealand

Penguin Books Ltd, Registered Offices:
Harmondsworth, Middlesex, England

First published in the United States of America by
Viking Penguin, a division of Penguin Books USA Inc., 1988
Published in Penguin Books 1989

1   3   5   7   9   10   8   6   4   2

LIBRARY OF CONGRESS CATALOGING-IN-PUBLICATION DATA
Marnham, Patrick.
    Trail of havoc: in the steps of Lord Lucan/Patrick Marnham.
    Reprint. Previously published: New York, N.Y., U.S.A.: Viking, 1988,
©1987.
    Includes index.
    ISBN 0 - 451 - 82208 - 0
1. Murder — England — London — Case studies.   2. Lucan, Richard John
Bingham, Earl of, 1934- .   3. Missing persons — England — Case
studies.   I. Title.
[HV6535.G6L6546   1989]   364.1′523′0942132 — dc 19   88 – 7992

Printed in the United States of America
Set in Garamond
Map by Andrew Farmer

To my friend 'the Inspector'

The single body on the drawing room carpet ... is more horrible and, indeed, more interesting than a dozen bullet-ridden corpses down Raymond Chandler's mean city streets ... [It is the] contrast between order, normality, hierarchy and the dreadful and contaminating irruption of violent death.

P. D. James

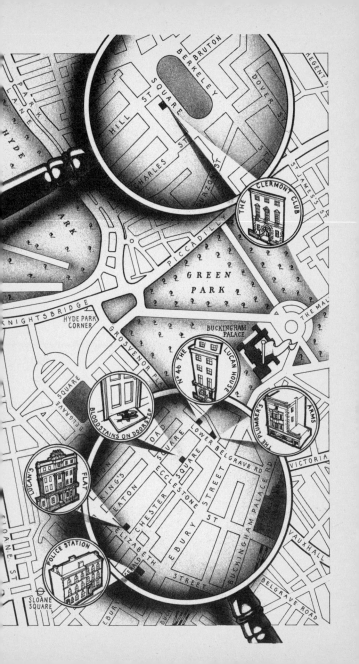

Contents

Acknowledgements

For the account of the social background to the Charge of the Light Brigade at Balaclava, I have relied on *The Reason Why* by Cecil Woodham-Smith. For the pattern of social events in London during the 1950s I have consulted Andrew Barrow's indispensable record, *Gossip*. All who write about the murder which took place at 46 Lower Belgrave Street in November 1974 are indebted to the pioneering work of James Fox.

I also wish to thank those who agreed to talk to me but who do not wish to be named.

P. M.

Paris, August 1987

Grateful acknowledgement is made to the following individuals and publishers for permission to quote copyright material: Chaim Bermant for an extract from an article that appeared first in the *Jewish Chronicle,* contributed under the pseudonym Ben Azai (pp. 136–7); the *Daily Telegraph* for an extract from an article by William Deedes (pp. 120–22); Tessa Sayle Agency for an extract from a song from *Oh, What a*

Lovely War!, published by Methuen, © 1965 Joan Littlewood Productions Ltd. (p.141); *The Times* for extracts from an article by Lord Shawcross (pp. 150-52); Auberon Waugh for an extract from an article first published in the *Spectator* (pp. 159-60).

The author and publishers also acknowledge with gratitude permission to reproduce the photographs included in this book: B B C Hulton Picture Library, 1, 2, 3; Camera Press, 8, 28, 35; Express Newspapers, 29; Press Association, 20, 34; Syndication International, 17, 18, 21, 22, 26, 36; Topham Picture Library, 6, 13, 19, 23, 24, 27, 30, 31, 32, 33.

Prologue

Lord Lucan is capable of hitting with enormous power.
His swing is inclined to get a bit rough but if I had the
pick of all the titled people who come to my school, I
would select Lord Lucan as the one potential champion.
Mr Leslie King, golf coach (1966)

Killing people on purpose is not as easy as it looks. Even
Dennis Nilsen, who confessed to the murder of fifteen
homosexuals, suffered the odd failure – the well-strangled
boy who, when Dennis was exhausted, popped up in the
bath to ask, 'What happened?'

But strangling requires considerable physical strength.
The most lethal tool for the average amateur killer is
probably the hand-gun. As long as a gun is pointed in the
right direction it frequently kills people. Even Ruth Ellis
managed to work a gun. The disadvantage of hand-guns
is that they are difficult to obtain, they leave numerous
clues and they make quite a noise – once heard never
forgotten. Silencers are even more difficult to obtain and
are virtually restricted to professional killers. There are
very few legitimate reasons for possessing a silencer. For

most amateur murderers a far more practical tool is a domestic implement.

Anyone rummaging through the kitchen drawer or tool box would find about half a dozen lethal weapons, most of them blades or bludgeons. But the blade too requires some skill if the victim is not to evade the pass. The only weapon that requires virtually no physical dexterity is the bludgeon. It is the classic offensive weapon of the enthusiastic amateur.

It is an unfortunate fact that although so many people remember the young lady who was bludgeoned to death in the basement of 46 Lower Belgrave Street on the evening of 7 November 1974, very few can recall her name. Who today would remember the violent end of Mrs Rivett had it not been for the identity of the man sought for her murder? In the public perception, that was the only memorable thing about her.

One can start with certain objective facts, in chronological order. The first indisputable event which can be established by the evidence of independent witnesses is the entry of the Countess of Lucan, a petite brunette, into the bar of the Plumber's Arms in Lower Belgrave Street at about 9.45 p.m. People were able to remember the time because of the manner of Lady Lucan's entry. She flung open the door and screamed. She was staggering and bleeding from head wounds and wearing a night-dress. She cried, 'Help me! Help me! I have just escaped from a murderer!' Then she began to weep. She went on to say, 'My children ... my children ... He's in the house ... He's murdered the nanny ... Help me!'

It says something about the times we live in that this desperate plea did not lead to a general exit in the direction of the house in question. A woman bursts in, 'head to toe in blood' and screaming that her children are in the hands of a murderer, and nobody moves an inch. Instead of setting out to rescue the children mentioned as being in this predicament, the barman and customers of the pub contented themselves with calling for the police and an ambulance, assisting Lady Lucan and trying to find out more about the event she spoke of. While Mrs Whitehouse, the wife of the head barman, tried to bandage Lady Lucan's head, her husband asked the questions. Although it must have seemed to everyone in the bar that important events were unfolding before their eyes, this was an illusion. In truth everything significant that could certainly be established had already taken place. The story which appeared just to have started was, in a sense, already over. The task remaining was merely to tell the story, to find out what had happened. It is a task which Mr Whitehouse commenced and which countless others have taken up, but one which remains unfulfilled even today. In due course Lady Lucan was taken by ambulance to the casualty department of St George's Hospital, Hyde Park Corner, about three minutes' drive away. A police van, call sign 'Echo Zero Fox', had been summoned by radio and directed to the Plumber's Arms. It arrived at the pub at 10.04.

When Police Sergeant Baker and Constable Beddick reached the solid front door of No. 46, some minutes later, they might have expected to find it open. Instead it was closed and they had to force it. The house was in darkness. The light of their torch showed blood streaks, still wet, on the wallpaper at the end of the hall. Sticking together, they descended to the basement and found a large pool of blood at the foot of the stairs. Were their truncheons drawn at this point? Did they expect to be confronted with a murderer, his bloody weapon still to hand? Still together, the officers left the basement and proceeded towards the top of the house. The stairs were in darkness. On the second floor the policemen found a room with a bedside light switched on. Here a bloodstained towel was draped across the pillow. On the floor above they found living people, three children, two of them asleep, the oldest, a 10-year-old girl, awake and standing by her bed. The volume of the T V set in the room had been turned right up.

Resuming their search of the house, Sergeant Baker and Constable Beddick returned to the basement. The bulb for the light in the kitchen had been removed, and they replaced it. This was a mistake, as it might have carried fingerprints. They then saw that there was a second pool of blood by the foot of the stairs and that broken cups and saucers were lying in it. Passing into the adjoining breakfast room they found a US mailbag, made of canvas, with the top folded over but not closed. There was blood leaking from the bag, and an arm was hanging out of it. Inside was the body of a young woman with severe head injuries. She had been doubled up and placed in the bag head and feet first. Her body was warm, but the policemen could find no pulse. At 10.20 detectives arrived and shortly afterwards, in an ante-room off the hall, they picked up a length of bloodstained lead piping, about 9 inches long, bound in surgical tape, which was twisted and bent.

At St George's Hospital the casualty officer who examined Veronica Lucan found that she had suffered seven scalp wounds and cuts inside the mouth and that she was in a state of severe shock. She was to remain in hospital for six days. At 6 o'clock the following morning the police took a statement from Lady Lucan, in which she accused her husband John of murdering Mrs Rivett and of attempting to murder her. That is the first sequence of objective facts.

The police explanation of these events was presented at the inquest into Sandra Rivett's death, and it can be summarized as follows. On 7 November 1974 the Earl of Lucan, aged 39, a professional gambler on a long losing streak, with heavy debts, who was separated from his wife and obsessed by his children, decided to change the course of his life. After nightfall he gained access to the London house where his family still lived and concealed himself in the basement. He was armed with a length of lead piping and he had removed the light bulb. It was three weeks, to the day, short of his eleventh wedding anniversary.

It was his wife's custom to make a cup of tea every evening at about 9 o'clock. At the expected time a slight female figure descended the unlit stairs to the basement, carrying a tea tray. As she reached the bottom step, Lord Lucan leaned over the banister and started to beat her to death. While engaged in inserting her body into a canvas bag which he had for this purpose, Lucan heard the sound of another person descending the stairs and calling, 'Sandra, Sandra.' He recognized the voice of his wife. But for the fact that she was not singing 'La donna è mobile', he might have been living through the last scene of *Rigoletto*. The slight female with the tea tray had not, after all, been his wife, Veronica, but Sandra Rivett, the children's nanny, who usually had Thursday evenings off. Undeterred by the fact that he had killed the wrong woman, Lucan waited until Veronica passed through the darkened hall and then launched another attack. He failed again. This time his victim fought back. He managed to land seven blows to the skull, but his wife did not weaken. So, dropping the lead piping, by now seriously distorted, he attempted to throttle Veronica by thrusting his gloved hand into her mouth. This gave her an opportunity to insert herself between his legs and grip his testicles. The fight ended. Both parties were exhausted. They agreed to talk things over. Lucan helped his wife upstairs and went to the bathroom to fetch a towel. She saw her chance and rushed out of the house for help. By the time the police arrived he had vanished into the night.

Only two people have admitted any contact with Lord Lucan since he disappeared. The first was his mother, who arrived at the house in Lower Belgrave Street at 10.45. She said that her son had telephoned her and asked her to go the house where there had been a 'terrible catastrophe'. That night the Dowager Countess of Lucan took her grandchildren to sleep in her house in St John's Wood. She was accompanied by P. C. Beddick. Shortly after midnight the telephone rang. It was Lucan again, inquiring about the children. He declined to speak to the police, said he would call them in the morning and rang off.

The other person who spoke to Lucan that night was an old friend of his, Susan Maxwell-Scott, who lived at Grants Hill House, Uckfield, Sussex. She subsequently told the police that she had been disturbed shortly after 11 p.m. by the front-door bell. It was Lord Lucan. She gave him a Scotch and he repeated the story he had already told his mother in the first telephone call he made to her: that, as he was passing the house, he had seen through the basement window a man attacking his wife; that he had let himself in with his key and gone downstairs, where he had slipped in a pool of blood. The intruder had escaped. His wife was hysterical. She said that Sandra had been murdered and accused him of hiring the man to kill her. Mrs Maxwell-Scott said that Lucan wrote two letters while he was in her house and telephoned his mother. He left at about 1.15 a.m. saying that he had to get back to 'clear things up'.

By far the most important evidence turned up in Newhaven on the Sunday afternoon, three days after the murder. It was a car belonging to Mr Michael Stoop, a friend of Lucan, which Lucan had borrowed about two weeks previously. The inside was heavily bloodstained and the boot contained a length of lead piping 2 feet long. It was bound in adhesive tape in the same way as the weapon found in Lady Lucan's house. The car had been parked in Newhaven since early on the morning of the day following the murder.

After forensic examination of the bloodstains in the house and the car, and the two lengths of lead piping, the police case against Lord Lucan was virtually complete.

PART ONE

The Man who Wanted his Children Back

I went downstairs again to Mummy's room at about 8.40. I asked Mummy where Sandra was and Mummy said she was downstairs making tea.

After a while Mummy said she wondered why Sandra was so long. It was before the *News* came on at 9 p.m. I said I would go downstairs to see what was keeping her, but Mummy said, no, she would go down. She left the bedroom door open, but there was no light in the hall. Just after Mummy left the room I heard a scream. It sounded as though it came from a long way away. I thought perhaps the cat had scratched Mummy and she had screamed. I was not frightened. I went to the door and called Mummy but there was no answer and I left it.

From the statement of Lady Frances Bingham

CHAPTER ONE

Above the Law

It is almost impossible to picture the deference, the adulation, the extraordinary privileges accorded to the nobility in the first half of the nineteenth century. A peer was above the law which applied to other men.

Cecil Woodham-Smith, *The Reason Why*

The general who led the Charge of the Light Brigade in 1854, the 7th Earl of Cardigan, was an unusually stupid man and notoriously unsuited to military command. Shortly after purchasing his first regiment, the 15th Hussars, he behaved in such an insulting manner to his own officers that he was removed from his position and retired on half-pay. It was a mark of his extraordinary incompetence that such a disgrace should have fallen on one of the most privileged men in England. It was a mark of just how great that privilege was that the disgraced Earl should, through influence at Court and against the wishes of both the Duke of Wellington and the Commander-in-Chief of the Army, have been allowed to purchase the command of another cavalry regiment within two years of his downfall. From then on Lord Cardigan never looked back. He became one of the most vilified men in England, and he thrived on it. Throughout his charmed life he had an unconquerable conviction of his rightness and superiority. On being justly criticized in the *Morning Chronicle* he threatened to horse-whip the paper's leader writer. Years later he prosecuted a brother officer for criminal libel, without success. All England considered him ridiculous when he dressed the Hussars of his new regiment in operatic, cherry-coloured, skin-tight pants. By way of response he paid his men to stand in the street and salute him. He insulted and bullied his junior officers. He fought a duel using a pistol with a rifled barrel and a hair trigger against an opponent using a conventional and less accurate weapon. After he had purchased his second regiment there were public petitions to remove him from command once more. When he was admonished by the Commander-in-Chief of the Army he ignored the letters. For wounding his opponent in the duel he was charged with intent to murder and *The Times* danced an editorial jig of hate: 'Let his head be cropped, let him be put on an oatmeal diet, let him labour on the treadmill . . .' In the event the Crown mysteriously failed to prepare an adequate case and Lord Cardigan was acquitted by the House of Lords, the jury of his peers. On the night of his acquittal he appeared at Drury Lane Theatre, and at the sight of him the audience rioted. Taking heart, he outraged popular feeling further by having one of his Hussars flogged on a Sunday in the building used as a regimental chapel. Following this incident he was pursued by the London mob and forced to drive around in a carriage with the blinds down. Feeling that he had not been paid the honour due to him, he asked for, and was refused, the Lord Lieutenancy of Northamptonshire. He then demanded the highest order in the kingdom, the Garter, as compensation. This too was refused him, three times. Despite everything, he continued in command of his regiment, and on the outbreak of the Crimean War he was promoted to brigadier-general and placed in command of the Light Cavalry Brigade. His immediate superior was his brother-in-law, George Bingham, 3rd Earl of Lucan, the major-general in command of the Cavalry Division. It was a notorious fact that the two men could not stand the sight of each other.

If Lord Cardigan was an anachronism, the sort of aristocrat you had only to look at to wonder about the address of Dr Guillotin, Lord Lucan should have enjoyed a very different reputation. Where Cardigan was stupid, Lucan was intelligent. He had never approved his brother-in-law's reinstatement in the Army; Lucan called Cardigan 'the feather-bed soldier'; and when Cardigan was given command of his second regiment Lucan said that Cardigan was 'not fit to command an escort'. Lucan had been born into a family originally famous for its warrior-like qualities, ferocity and cruelty, but noted subsequently for artistic interests and talents. His grandmother was a painter whose pictures were admired by Louis XVI and Marie Antoinette. His aunt was a famous beauty who became Countess Spencer. His mother and father eloped and were able to marry only after his elder sister had been born and after his mother's first marriage had been dissolved by Act of Parliament. They were regarded as a model of romantic imprudence. As a little boy George Bingham had been 'frank, open and affectionate'. His father, when young, had been regarded as one whose talents would lead him to outshine Pitt or Fox. On leaving school, George Bingham joined the Army, rose swiftly through the purchase system and was soon considered one of the most promising and intelligent officers in the service. Peel told Wellington that Bingham was 'a fine, high-spirited young fellow', and Wellington 'thought well of him'. But there had none the less been an unfortunate change in his character. The affectionate little boy had grown up into a harsh man with an appalling temper. He was a throwback to his ferocious ancestors. And he had developed one characteristic fatal to his own happiness – he had an obsessive sense of grievance against the world. He was a harsh commander of men, but his qualities became obvious to all only during the period of his life when he decided to take an interest in his Irish estates.

The Bingham connection with Ireland had begun in the reign of Queen Elizabeth I, when three Bingham brothers distinguished themselves as soldiers of fortune. One of them, Richard Bingham, became military governor of Connaught, the western province of Ireland, where his character is remembered today. It was he who ordered that all Spaniards shipwrecked on the coast after the Armada should have their throats cut, a massacre which even now is invariably attributed to the unprompted savagery of the people of Connaught. Over the years the Binghams continued to occupy even larger estates, by right of conquest. They concentrated on Mayo and established their seat at Castlebar. Like most English landowners they were chiefly interested in their land as a source of income. It was because the income was so low that George Bingham, the future 3rd Earl of Lucan, decided to devote himself to the Irish property in 1837. So he left his regiment and turned to farming and politics. Two years later he inherited his father's title.

Lord Lucan's life in Ireland is almost as marked by scandal as was Lord Cardigan's life in England. Shortly after his arrival he quarrelled both with his Irish agent and with the English officers garrisoned at Castlebar. Such was the violence of his quarrel with the agent that Lucan was removed from the Castlebar bench by the Lord Chancellor of Ireland. Lucan's response was to raise this piffling matter in the House of Lords, which debated it three times. The

Lords declined to intervene, so Lucan decided to revive the ancient manorial court. He would abolish the Queen's court in Castlebar and dispense his own justice. In Mayo, at least, he would literally be above the law. Indeed, 'the law' would be Lucan. His solicitors told him that it was no longer possible to do this, so he appealed to the Lord Chancellor of England, who agreed with his solicitors. By the end of the thing Lucan had gained nothing but had quarrelled with half the town of Castlebar.

Ireland was at the time on the brink of the potato famine. Eight million people were assembled on the island at a density higher than existed in China and relying for all their food on the potato. The Irish were the poorest people in Europe, and the poorest of the Irish lived in Mayo. These people hated their landlords, and the landlords held their tenants in contempt. In this situation Lucan decided that the best solution was eviction. The land would be cleared of the teeming, starving masses and farmed in a modern manner. Begged to show mercy, Lucan declared that he 'did not intend to breed paupers to pay priests'. He was prepared to spend money on his land, far above its rental value; in return he would drive the people off it. The potato crop failed in 1845, 1846, 1847 and 1848. By then the Irish population was reduced by 2.5 million people. Throughout all this, Lord Lucan carried out his policy of evictions. The tenants and their children were thrown off the land to die in the ditch. Shelters were pulled down on the heads of those too weak to move. Lucan became known as 'the Exterminator'. In this situation the only chance left for those starving to death was the workhouse, and at Castlebar the workhouse closed its gates. Its chairman was Lord Lucan. People died in hundreds outside. Asked to explain himself in the House of Lords, Lucan said that there was no money to pay for relief since the tenants, who were starving, had failed to pay their rates. He faced his

critics with irritation and considered himself mis-
understood. He may have been more intelligent than Lord
Cardigan, but he was every bit as self-righteous. Lucan
had intended to impose on his Irish estates a model system
of agriculture. He succeeded only in making himself one
of the most hated men in Ireland and in causing the deaths
of thousands of those who were supposed to benefit from
his plan. In manner he became chronically aggressive. The
government in London, which kept an admirably cool
head over the plight of Ireland, was not unduly disturbed
by his conduct. And when, five years later, England
embarked an army for the Crimea and Lord Lucan was
given command of the Cavalry Division – seventeen years
after leaving his regiment – it was said that he had won
this distinction for the qualities he showed in Ireland:
'ruthlessness, energy, disregard for sentiment and contempt for public opinion'. Ireland's danger had been
Lucan's opportunity.

The Charge of the Light Brigade, led by Lord Cardigan on
Lord Lucan's orders, became one of the most famous
disasters in British military history. It is remembered for
the discipline and courage of the men who trusted their
officers and charged the Russian guns to certain death, and
for the bone-headed obstinacy of the quarrelling brothers-
in-law who led them. It was the culminating act of
arrogance in two brutal lives. At the end of it all, Lord
Lucan carried the blame. He had set out for the Crimea
with high hopes of military glory. His moment came. He
intervened in the battle, destroyed half the division he led
and covered his name in disgrace. And it was all completely
unfair. The orders he had received from Lord Raglan, the
Commander-in-Chief, were ambiguous.

When news of the disaster reached England, Lucan was
recalled and asked to resign. He was refused the court-

martial which might have cleared his name, and he had to endure the taunts of Lord Cardigan, who had been mobbed as a hero because he had led the charge.

Cardigan, never one to miss an opportunity of this sort, rode in procession to the Guildhall amid cheering crowds, wearing his Balaclava uniform. He ignored *The Times*, which said that the spectacle had 'a strong hint of Madame Tussaud's about it'. Lord Lucan, generally known as 'Lord Look-on' – even though he had been wounded during the Charge – did not ignore criticism in the *Daily News*. He sued for libel and lost.

Who could have foreseen the curious way in which certain themes of that old story were to be repeated 120 years later? In the events that followed the murder of Sandra Rivett, a peer was committed for trial on a charge of felony; the Crown became involved in his prosecution and mishandled it; a magistrate was dismissed; violence was used against a journalist; there were elopements; an Earl of Lucan was regarded as a 'throwback'; a group of well-connected people considered themselves to be above the law; and private prosecution for criminal libel was revived. Through the mist of time and the smoke of the battlefield one sees the cavalrymen of Balaclava, their sword arms rising and falling as they hack down their enemies. And when the smoke cleared, a stupid man was treated as a hero, and an intelligent one as a fool. And so a sense of grievance, of a wrong unrighted, of an insult unavenged, was born. And a fatal belief grew up that only by decisive action could life's problems be overcome: action – even outside the law – however swift or savage.

CHAPTER TWO

Not Criminals but Outlaws

As late as 1941, Lieutenant-Colonel Ralph Bingham, DSO, a great-great-grandson of the hero of the Irish Famine and Balaclava (and uncle to John), could write in a letter to *The Times*: 'Never was the old school tie and the best that it stands for more justified than it is today. Our new armies are being officered by classes of society who are new to the job. The middle, lower-middle and working classes are now receiving the King's commission. These classes, unlike the old aristocratic and feudal classes who led the old Army, have never had "their people" to consider. They have never had anyone to think of but themselves. This aspect of life is completely new to them and they have very largely fallen down on it in their capacity as Army officers.'

Lieutenant-Colonel Bingham failed to carry his point. He was at the time in command of an officers' training unit. His letter caused a public outcry. Winston Churchill said he was a 'goose', and Bingham was relieved of his post. It is possible that this letter gave Evelyn Waugh an idea for Lieutenant Hooper, one of the characters in *Brideshead Revisited*; it certainly underlined the changes that

had occurred in society since the days when the 3rd Earl of
Lucan had fended for 'his people'. But things actually got
worse for the rich and the nobility after the Second World
War. The values of Ralph Bingham vanished with the
arrival of peace. The new classes left their temporary commissions and took over the country. The siege lasted for
six years, reaching its height in 1950, when Earl Peel was
fined £25,000 merely for spending more than the Labour
government would allow on repairing his stately home.
With the election of a Conservative government in the
following year, and promises of an end of austerity, the
stage was set for a last big spree. If the children of the
'right' people could no longer enjoy themselves in the old
way, then they would just have to enjoy themselves in
whatever way they could. The gossip columnists called
these young people the 'Chelsea set', a phrase that laced
snobbery with a faint flavour of criminality.

Unlike the youth of the 1960s, those who were young
ten years earlier believed in the importance of rules because
the whole fun of life lay in breaking them. They took
themselves a great deal less seriously than the grim-faced
rigorists of drugs, sex and freedom. The classlessness of
the flower children would not have been at all to their
taste. The 1950s were a great age for 'cads'. It was a time
of fortune hunters and elopements. People wanted a rest
from the 'goody-goody' days of national sacrifice. They
found bounders who carried off heiresses to their taste. In
the Fifties there was an interesting age when a girl was too
old for statutory rape but too young to leave her father's
house without permission. Girls of 18 and 19 became an
almost irresistible target for their admirers. It was a time of
post-war euphoria when it was admirable to be rich, a
compassionate morality was less fashionable than it is today
and public opinion was sympathetic towards those who
were forced by a lack of money to take short cuts. Everyone

was hoping to ride the crest of the wave. For the rich there was the stockmarket and the expanding post-war economy; for the poor there` was the removal of hire-purchase restrictions and the promise of easy credit. Freshly expelled from their public schools, the cads took to this world like pike released into a pond full of succulent duckling.

Two of the most highly publicized adventures concerned Jimmy Goldsmith and Dominick Elwes. In 1953 a 'penniless Old Etonian', James Goldsmith, fell in love with the 17-year-old heiress to a Bolivian tin fortune, Isabel Patino. Her multi-millionaire father, Señor Antenor Patino, pursued the couple to the Scottish border, but he was too late. In May 1954 Mrs Goldsmith died suddenly while expecting a baby. The little girl lived. In September the baby was kidnapped in Paris by her grandparents. Her father got her back only after a court case.

Another young man, Dominick Elwes, quickly achieved 'social prominence', which meant that he was frequently seen at parties which attracted the attention of Fleet Street gossip writers. He went to a fancy-dress ball dressed as a cowboy and danced with Little Red Riding Hood, who turned out to be Princess Margarethe of Sweden. Princess Margarethe broke off a romance with the nightclub pianist Robin Douglas-Home, who consoled himself at a dance given for Tessa Kennedy, 'the wealthy god-daughter of Princess Marina'. In due course Tessa Kennedy eloped with Dominick Elwes. Dominic and Tessa put on a show every bit as good as the Goldsmiths'. It started in 1957 with a High Court injunction prohibiting Tessa, then 18, from leaving the country and prohibiting Elwes, 26, from marrying her. This was irresistible and the lovers promptly went on the run. They failed to get married in Scotland. A second injunction was issued, ordering Elwes to return his child-bride-to-be. Shortly afterwards Dominick and Tessa were reported to be heading for the Dutch West Indies, but they were eventually married in Havana. Six weeks after that they were discovered stranded in a Florida flat, broke and in need of food. Money must have been found because they were married again in New York, and Dominick came home with Tessa, on the liner *Liberté*, to face the music. When the ship docked in Southampton it was met by the High Court tipstaff. That evening Elwes began an indeterminate jail sentence to purge his contempt. He was released after two weeks – in time to be married to Tessa for the third time. Every move made by the lovers was attended by press coverage, which was masterminded by David Wynne-Morgan, a friend of Elwes who was then a reporter on the *Daily Express*.

Ian Maxwell-Scott was another young man who married against parental opposition. His wife, Susan, was the daughter of Sir Andrew Clark, QC, who said of Mr Maxwell-Scott: 'The fellow is not to my taste. He has no proper job. He is a gambler. I prefer the man who does an honest day's work to any amount of nobility or family names.' This was a reference to the fact that Maxwell-Scott was both a cousin of the Duke of Norfolk and a croupier. He was banned from Susan's twenty-first birthday party but married her three months later. The priest who married them was Monsignor Valentine Elwes, Dominick's uncle. Sir Andrew did not attend the wedding. The lives of these three young men, Goldsmith, Elwes and Maxwell-Scott, were eventually to be linked by a less romantic thread.

Elopements were one way of 'taking the law into your own hands', but there were others. At just the time when Dominick Elwes and Tessa Kennedy were leaving for Cuba, John Aspinall appeared at Marylebone Magistrates' Court charged with 'keeping a common gaming house' at a flat in Hyde Park Street. Twenty-one other people were charged with him, including his mother, Lady Osborne, and Lord Willoughby de Eresby. The defendants were acquitted of the charge in March 1958. It was a strong point in their defence that there was no evidence that they had used the address 'habitually', a necessary ingredient of the offence of keeping a common gaming house. It was, of course, a notorious fact at that time that illegal gaming always took place at a different address every night. The person running the game moved on and the punters just had to find out where he had got to. When he was acquitted John Aspinall said, 'I have been giving parties since the age of ten. I am awfully fond of playing the host.' And Lady Osborne, known to some of her customers as 'Al Capone with the handbag', said, 'It is a poor thing if you can't have a private party in a private flat without the police coming.' This complaint struck a popular chord. Nobody disputed that gaming had been taking place at the Aspinalls' parties; too many policemen had been peering through too many chinks in the curtains to deny that. But Aspinall having been acquitted on a technicality, there was public criticism of the police for spying on private houses, and two years later the law was changed to allow gaming in England. Aspinall, a man of action, had first ignored the rules and then changed them. Life for him in future would be a little less fun but much more profitable.

But before the law was changed Society's extra-legal activities had also attracted the attention of more serious criminals. It became chic for Chelsea girls to have at least one walk-out with a boy from the East End. Jewel thieves, especially 'cat burglars' – all jewel thieves were 'cat bur-glars' to their admirers – were adorned with the status of master craftsmen. A racket developed whereby daughters of wealthy parents, knowing that the family treasures were safely insured, would do the homework for their boyfriends. More important, the heavy mob took to visiting a lot of the amateur gaming houses. The approach was always the same; in return for a cut, they *'wouldn't* break the place up'. Then, in order to ensure they were getting a 'reasonable' cut, they would maintain a permanent presence. Before long they would be running the game and shortly after that the game was bent.

One of the most prominent members of the heavy mob was Frank 'Charlie' Mitchell, later to become notorious as the 'Mad Axeman', who disappeared in unexplained circumstances in the mid-1960s. The novelist Robin Cook, who was at the time running several illegal tables in Chelsea, will never forget the visits that Charlie paid him. Charlie was a man of enormous strength and somewhat intimidating appearance. ' 'Ere, Robin' was the simple nature of his usual greeting, and on hearing these two words Mr Cook's heart would sink. One morning the doorbell rang early and repeatedly. 'Morning, Robin! 'Ere, you want a motor?'

'No, thanks, Charlie, I've already . . .'

'Good. It's outside, £500, and I'll need cash.' Charlie gestured towards a gleaming American model, the most conspicuous object in the street. When he had pocketed the cash Charlie added one helpful detail. 'I wouldn't leave it around like that if I was you, Robin. It's hot.'

On another occasion Mr Cook remembers that he had managed to acquire from his father, without his father's knowledge, two cases of 'exceptionally fine claret'. The entertainment of the punters was always a problem. If they were going to lay their money out, they must be kept happy and they had all been brought up to recognize good wine. Here was the problem solved for the week. The doorbell rang while the wooden cases and straw packing were still in the hall. 'Evening, Robin! 'Ere, that looks like good claret.'

'What? Oh, that. No, no, absolute rubbish I'm afraid. Bought a dud lot.'

'Are you trying to be funny or something, Robin? Fink I don't know good claret when I see it? It's still got the straw round it. 'Ere, Joe, pop these in the boot, could you? Fanks very much, Robin.'

Matters were not always as cordial, however. The East End was not accustomed to running straight games. The idea was to tempt rich mugs into bent games. Since all the games were illegal anyway, there was no form of supervision. Just as in the three-card trick played in the street, there had to be a period of encouragement when the mugs were allowed to win a bit. After that the house won. If something went wrong and one of the punters won, he had to be seen to be paid. For those who *were* paid the problem was to keep the money. Archie McNair-Scott and Alexander Plunket Greene had a difficult time one night in a dark mews after a handsome win: one had to cover the other's exit with his car headlamps.

When the Kray twins moved in and started Esmeralda's Barn in Knightsbridge it was not a very satisfactory situation for the straightforward punter who liked to play the tables. But until the law was changed in 1960 there was no alternative and so, in the 1950s in London, close links were forged between the wealthy young people who enjoyed indoor gambling and some of the roughest mobs in the East End. Even after the law was changed, when bent gaming houses went out of business, one temptation to extra-legal solutions remained. English law will not assist a creditor who wishes to recover the profits of a wager. This is a standing invitation to criminality. If the most important financial transaction in which a group of men engage is unenforceable at law, it is inevitable, when someone refuses or is unable to meet his commitments, that sooner or later others will consider extra-legal means of collecting the money. In this area at least Chelsea could find a use for the specialists of the East End even after gambling was legalized.

There were, of course, other ways of having fun. Elwes, who had failed in his youthful attempt to gain an Army commission, set off for Hungary in 1956 to fight in the uprising. Later, in 1965, an RAF officer was court-martialled for passing military secrets to Elwes that were pertinent to the civil war in the Yemen. Britain was officially neutral in this war, but Colonel David Stirling, the officer who had founded the SAS, was helping the royalist forces, and Elwes was helping Colonel Stirling. It was a call to arms of a sort. It was another adventure. It was just right for young men who would have hotly denied that they were criminals but who were proud to call themselves outlaws.

CHAPTER THREE

The House Without a Clock

I've come to close your door, my handsome, my darling,
I've come to close your door, and never come again.
The shadow on the ceiling will not be mine, my darling,
So if you wake in terror, cry some other name.
      from Frances Bellerby, 'Bereft Child's First Night'

John Bingham married Veronica Duncan in November 1963. In the view of his friends, the marriage had been a mistake from the start. In his case there must have been a strong attraction; in hers, in her own words, 'I was looking for a god, and he was a dream figure.' It is noticeable that Veronica Lucan rarely smiles in her photographs and that John Lucan rarely smiles in photographs taken with her. As a couple, they usually seemed to be glaring at the world, handsomely.

They had been introduced by Veronica's sister, Christina, who had married a wealthy friend of Lucan, Bill Shand Kydd. Veronica's wedding took place in the same year and at the same church as her sister's. She and John were married one month after becoming engaged. Two months after the marriage Bingham's father died suddenly and he became the 7th Earl of Lucan. He had until then worked in a merchant bank. His chief recreations had been bridge and golf. But with the money he inherited on his father's death he was able to set up house in Lower Belgrave Street and start on a new career as a professional gambler. It was a romantic fantasy that his more realistic wife could not share. Lucan gradually lost touch with his former friends, even with John Wilbraham, best man at his wedding. His new friends were mostly people with the same interests. Winning a big bet can be even more disastrous than losing one. Lucan's 'belief' in his luck, his professional qualification, started after he had won £20,000 at chemin de fer in 1964. That was when he was given the nickname 'Lucky'. The next day he handed in his notice at the bank. Later he won a backgammon tournament, which confirmed his unfortunate belief.

From the start it was an unpromising situation. He had inherited £250,000 and a private income from various family trusts. He had also inherited 600 stroppy tenants in Co. Mayo, 100 acres in Staines, occupied by a golf club, as well as smaller amounts of property in London and Rhodesia. The private income that Lucan enjoyed after his father's death was sufficient to stake him as a gambler but insufficient to support heavy losses.

Quite quickly the Lucans acquired three small children. After the birth of his son, George, Lucan was in high spirits. Because he wore such smart suits he was sometimes mistaken in the hospital for a consultant. He took the opportunity to do a ward round, examining fever charts and asking patients how they were feeling. But that was an untypically light-hearted moment. Keeping up appearances in Belgravia while leading a frivolous life is a grim business, and Lucan was determined to keep up appearances. In these circumstances his wife gradually became worried and impatient. She also began to complain. As she did so, she lost the sympathy of Lucan's friends.

Veronica Duncan's father, an army officer, had died when she was young. Her mother had then taken the children to South Africa, where Veronica grew up an intense, competitive little girl, over-anxious to be accepted and to succeed. She was at one point in her childhood treated by a psychiatrist. This was an experience she had in common with her future husband. Her mother eventually married again, and the family moved back to England. Her stepfather took over the tenancy of a hotel near Basingstoke in Hampshire – the place which one of Lucan's friends later referred to as 'a pub on the way back from Ascot'. The girls were sent to St Swithin's School in Winchester. It was a typical middle-class upbringing. But Veronica was not confident. She was smaller than her younger sister and for some reason had been taught that smallness was, as in puppies, a sign of ill-breeding. Breeding became an obsession with her. In any event, after her marriage she made herself an expert on social precedence. The question of breeding went very deep. When she was asked how her skull had been able to withstand the type of brutal attack which had killed Sandra Rivett she replied, 'Good breeding.'

Apart from a lack of social confidence, Veronica Lucan was disinclined to accept the conventional role of a gambler's wife. She was the more intelligent of the two and she had a sharp tongue. This did not win her many friends either. 'The trouble was that she wanted it both ways,' said one. 'She complained about his gambling all the time but she also insisted on being present while he did it.' So the way was made ready for a serious disagreement. The chosen battleground was to be the Clermont Club.

There is about the drama of 7 November 1974 a certain

lack of topographical invention. Lucan established his alibi outside the Clermont Club in Berkeley Square. The crime was committed in Lower Belgrave Street. One of those who expected Lucan for dinner at the Clermont Club later that evening lived behind Lucan's house in a mews flat in Eaton Row. Lucan himself had taken a flat in Elizabeth Street, two blocks to the west. The police who were called to the scene of the crime came from Gerald Road police station, which leads off Elizabeth Street. After the crime Lucan drove to the house of friends near Uckfield. Uckfield had been Veronica Lucan's first home. When she returned from South Africa she had gone to live near Basingstoke. Basingstoke was also the birthplace and home of Sandra Rivett. The same place names keep recurring, insignificantly. How much disbelief can be evoked by investigators or prosecuting counsel when a suspect pleads coincidence? How sinister it can be made to seem. Here is an example of the unimportance of coincidence.

At the centre of this unmagical mystery tour is the boundary between Mayfair and Belgravia. The passing of the 1960 Betting and Gaming Act had enabled John Aspinall to dismiss his removal firm; henceforth his tables were legal and could be set up in a permanent house. In 1962 Aspinall opened the Clermont Club in one of the most beautiful houses in London, designed by William Kent, at 44 Berkeley Square. It was an oddity of the club that it had no clock. Inside the club time stopped. This was a pleasing addition to the gambler's fantasy. After the raunchy days of the Fifties, the Clermont provided style. To his tables Aspinall was now able to attract the richest and most reckless gamblers in the country. He also attracted people who lacked the self-discipline to control their gambling and who quickly became dependent on him. Among the latter was Lord Lucan, eight years his junior.

In the days before the 1960 Act, Aspinall had been able

to run his games pretty well as he chose. He could take part in them himself; he could, if he wished, extend enough credit to ruin any man who chose to pay. There were no legal constraints. After the 1960 Act such ploys were banned. It was a regulated and less adventurous world, and one in which professional gamblers became an endangered species. Casino chains and multinational bookmakers know who the professional winners are and take steps to exclude them. What they want are inexperienced mugs or rich idiots, and there are plenty of both. Professional gamblers prosper by exercising skill in those games of chance which contain a sufficient element of skill – backgammon possibly, poker and the horses. Once they start getting too good at it they find it difficult to get their bets on. So, as a self-styled 'professional' winner, John Lucan was already an anachronism. Once he settled down to lose, of course, he became a much more welcome figure. And when he could no longer meet his debts, he became positively useful. With his name and background he was the perfect 'house player', a humiliating role for one of nature's outlaws. This slow decline took place over nine years. The capital was replaced by loans, and the debts mounted steadily, and his luck went from bad to worse. For Hope it was a dance of death which took its tempo from the drumming fingers and tapping feet of his deeply unimpressed wife, who accompanied him to the Clermont night after night. In the world of chance, where time stood still, a man and a woman picked their marriage to pieces.

From the point of view of an interested onlooker, there was nothing very amusing about the spectacle. One of those who came under Aspinall's spell, and escaped, has described the experience. 'We found ourselves, little by little, all spinning around Aspinall, and unable to deal with our lives in the way he was able to deal with his. He had the advantage of different values. His values were unlike other people's — a tiger's values, I suppose. He didn't regard people very much. If you went into the club and he came up to chat and then said, "Sit down," you did. And then of course you started to play. You were under the spell, within the aura. Once I said, "No." From that moment, Aspinall could see that I was no longer under the spell. He could see it. It was like cutting a cord. The more people were drawn in, the more lost they became. It led to ruin for many people. He had a very powerful influence on a lot of people. And in some cases it helped to destroy them. If people didn't walk away, eventually they got snuffed out. There was one chap up from Devon. He'd inherited £100,000. He lost the money in two nights. He sold his farm and paid up. When people asked Aspinall about it he just said the chap was an idiot for paying up. I don't know what would have have happened to him if he hadn't paid. Aspinall sometimes looked after people who went broke. For instance, when he eventually sold the Clermont to Playboy, he got a lot of people off their bills. But the pervading atmosphere was destructive.'

To this destructive atmosphere Lucan returned night after night, week after week, for eleven years, munching his smoked salmon and lamb cutlets, losing his fortune and stubbornly insisting on his skill and his luck. If Lord Lucan ate four lamb cutlets a day, for four days a week, for forty weeks a year, for eleven years, and if there are seven cutlets in a sheep, then he would by the end have dispatched 1,006 sheep. One of those who watched him doing it said that he gambled 'because gambling was simply the biggest thing in his life. He was not an imaginative person; he was two-dimensional. He had clear views but he never wasted time arguing. He started off as an independent person but then became more and more bound up with Aspinall. After he had lost his money he became a house player and that is a way of life in itself. It was a bloody easy way of life. Free meals, friends – it was a schoolboy way of life, really. As a gambler, of course, he was a fatalist. He probably thought he was destined to kill his wife.' Some gamblers consider it unlucky for their wives to sit at the gaming table. Perhaps by the end Lucan thought his dogged companion had become his ill luck.

Nobody knows how much money Lucan lost to Aspinall at the Clermont; it would probably be fair to say that Aspinall had most of it. The calculation is complicated by the extent to which Lucan was able to live on his income of £12,000 a year, the amount he won over the years and the amount he borrowed. But there was a serious change in his circumstances when Aspinall sold the Clermont Club to Playboy in 1972. Aspinall received £350,000. Lucan got an envelope full of his own bounced cheques. It was then that he started to sell the family silver. If he hadn't done that, he would not have been able to raise the £10,000 necessary to get him back into the club so that he could go on losing his money.

At the time of Lucan's disappearance he had sizeable overdrafts at four banks, amounting to £14,177 in all. In September 1974, the month when school fees in England have to be paid, Lucan visited a moneylender called Mr Charles Genese, who kept his hoard in Bexleyheath, Kent. Lucan asked to borrow £5,000. Mr Genese found him perfectly open about his debts, and eventually agreed to lend him £3,000 at 48 per cent per annum for six months with a surety. Lucan told Mr Genese that he intended to repay the loan after the sale at auction of some more family silver later in the year. Because the person standing surety was a friend of Lucan, he must have had every intention of repaying this debt. Obviously, at that stage, two months before the murder, he had no plans to disappear. The intended sale of family silver would not have helped him after his disappearance; he would have realized that in those circumstances his creditors would certainly have put in a receiver. The sale, which took place as planned at Christie's on 27 November, two weeks after the murder, raised £17,410. It would have been just about enough to repay the banks and Mr Genese.

The crisis in the Lucans' marriage had come eighteen months earlier, when he had walked out of the house in Lower Belgrave Street and had started proceedings to win custody of the children. By January 1973 the Lucans had been married for nine years. Their oldest child was eight, their youngest two. It was not a good time for Lucan to leave, but he and Veronica had started to quarrel in public, he had become a house player, he had lost all his money and he was continuing to play and continuing to lose. His wife found the situation impossible, and he could no longer bear to have her near him while he played. Asked about it, Lady Lucan said at the time: 'I think he did it on the spur of the moment. He simply decided he would like to live apart from me ... My husband and my children were my whole life and I am still fond of him.'

Lucan's feelings in the matter were evidently different. They seem to have developed from irritation to dislike and then to hatred. He was convinced that his wife was mentally ill. He was increasingly worried about the children. He employed private detectives to watch his wife, started to record his arguments with her on a concealed tape-recorder and mounted his campaign to regain custody of the children. He had moved into a basement flat in Elizabeth Street, and it was in the diminished surroundings of his new life that he conceived his master plan. He wanted his life to continue as before, but without his wife. She had to be erased. It was a fantasy, and it required a fantastic plan of action.

For a man newly separated from his wife and children a London basement, one of the traditional bolt-holes, can be the bleakest place. Here he finds the brave new world he longed for, the place where, having seized his independence, he can start to rebuild his life. All too often it is a world of takeaway cardboard pizzas, cartons of mouldy milk, flies on overripe fruit, unrinsed wine glasses, the portable television at the end of the bed, the overflowing suitcase of dirty clothes that never seems to get to the launderette, and the telephone that rings only when you are, at last, asleep.

Lucan was out of tune with the age. He opposed its levelling spirit, never more buoyant than it was in London in the 1960s. He was in the unusual position of being a young man whose elderly parents were more up to date than he was. The Lucan parents were examples of a particularly English type, 'left-wing old buffers'. His father, the 6th Earl, had commanded the Coldstream Guards and won the M C. Nevertheless, after the war he had joined Attlee's government as a junior minister for Commonwealth Relations, and for the last ten years of his life he was Chief Opposition Whip in the House of Lords. Furthermore it was Lucan's father who gave the historian Cecil Woodham-Smith access to the Bingham family papers and so enabled her to describe in detail the 3rd Earl's conduct in Mayo during the Irish Famine and his subsequent disgrace in the Crimea. *The Reason Why* by Cecil Woodham-Smith was published to loud acclaim in 1953, the year of the Coronation, when Lucan was aged 18. The question of the 3rd Earl's behaviour at Balaclava remained a sore point with John Lucan in later life. Lucan's mother was also an active member of the Labour Party. Their son, by contrast, was a disgrace; a professional gambler and barfly. His general attitude to life was closer to that of his uncle, Lieutenant-Colonel Ralph Bingham, Churchill's 'goose', than it was to that of his parents.

Although Lucan never expected to be given the extraordinary powers bestowed on his great-great-grandfather, the 3rd Earl, he did expect life to be lived largely on his own terms and he did consider that any obstacles to his convenience could quickly be overcome. And after the birth of his three children he had, for the first time in his life, an interest more serious than his own pleasure. Although the tactics he employed in his battle for custody were ruthless and odious, there seems no reason to doubt his sincerity. He was honestly convinced that his wife was unsuited to care for them. He knew that he would need evidence, so he tried to manufacture some. Before they separated Lucan had become convinced that Veronica was mentally ill and in need of treatment. As early as 1967, after their son was born, he had told his friends that Veronica was going mad. One day he took her for a drive in the country which ended at the gates of The Priory in Roehampton, an expensive nursing home that specializes in alcoholism and the care of the mentally ill. The doctors had been warned, but Veronica had not, and she refused to be admitted. For three years after that Veronica underwent psychiatric treatment for depression and anxiety. Then, in 1971, Lucan drove her to another mental hospital, this time with her consent. She walked inside but couldn't stand the sight of the place so ran out into the road and, by bus and taxi and on foot, made her way slowly home. For a few hours nobody knew where she was. She was upset and ill and she had disappeared. It is possible that this incident gave Lucan one of his occasional ideas.

During 1972 Lucan's concern with his children grew, to use his mother's words, into an 'obsession'. It was at this time that he bought the tape-recorder and started to play the tapes back to his friends. It was clear that he was provoking many of her outbursts and that he would start the tape-recorder only after Veronica had lost control. In January 1973, after Lucan had walked out, Veronica, who was already suffering from paranoia and hallucinations caused partly by the pills she had been prescribed, began to receive nuisance calls on an ex-directory number which only Lucan knew. When she went out of the house, private detectives followed her down the street. If she looked out of the window at night she would sometimes see her husband driving slowly past the house, wearing dark glasses. In a thoroughly sensible move she responded to this harassment in kind. She would walk past his basement 'to see him'. But she did not accept the reality of what had happened. She said once, 'I think he walked past here to see the children or maybe just to walk past the house where we lived. I think that is a strong indication we were both hoping to get back together again.' The last time she saw him it was exactly a fortnight before the night of the murder. She looked out of the window and there he was, sitting in his car, wearing his dark glasses.

The Lucans were not officially separated and there was no talk of divorce but, with the date for the custody hearing set for May, Lucan made a serious error. In March 1973 he sent his private detectives into action. Action at last! Lucan and his assistants followed the children and their nanny to Green Park, bundled the children into a taxi and took them back to 72A Elizabeth Street. The children stayed with him there in the weeks that remained before the case. It was an operational triumph, an intervention on the side of justice, a vigilante ploy that would decide events – or so Lucan thought.

In fact it was a blunder. There could hardly be a worse introduction to a custody hearing. Despite all Lucan's preparations, despite the secret tape-recordings and the expert medical evidence and the affidavits from so many friends and relations, Lucan lost the case. The judge considered him arrogant and untruthful and, on his own admission, lawless. There was also evidence that he had attacked Veronica and tried to strangle her, a suggestion which he denied but which was corroborated by one of the children's nannies. It was, in short, a classic custody disaster, the effective end of a marriage. The judge decided that Veronica could have custody of the children as long as she employed a nanny. That was as far as he would go in agreeing that she needed help. Lucan was left with a bill estimated at £40,000. The basement became bleaker than ever. His fellow fantasists were his only regular company; his only refuge was the house without a clock.

It is hard to overestimate the bitterness and alienation of a father in the position in which Lucan now found himself. The failure of his first 'decisive step' had not set him against the principle of action. It just made him think that his next attempt would have to be far more decisive and confirmed his view that there was no point in relying on the courts. An extra-legal initiative was called for. Many men, deprived of their children by a court, must have toyed with the attractions of mayhem. It does not take long for most to realize that if they wish to regain the company of their children, it is hardly very sensible to start by killing a judge. Once Lucan had worked his way through the court officials, both sets of solicitors, the psychiatrists and anyone else involved, he would have settled on the only remaining target: his wife. Some time after losing his custody case Lord Lucan made an entry in his diary that showed his weekly expenditure to be the following: rent £70, Nanny £25, wife £40, private detectives £40, Mercedes £85, loan from mother £75. This totalled over £17,000 a year. In addition he owed money to four banks and a moneylender; these loans were costing a further £15,000 a year. Furthermore he owed £40,000 for the legal costs after the custody case. His annual income was £12,000. Clearly, something would have to be done.

There have been more and less elaborate explanations of

his plans, which took over a year after the custody case to complete, but the essential theme is that in order to regain the company of his children Lucan had to cause his wife to disappear. This would involve her death and the disposal of her body. Lucan would have regarded the first stage as a technical problem. He was an officer in the Guards Reserve and he still kept up his pistol practice and his shooting. He had been trained in unarmed combat and he had numerous weapons at his disposal. He was much stronger than his wife.

The second problem was far more complicated, indeed notoriously difficult to overcome. But it was a vital part of the plan, for if Lucan was to be sure of regaining the children, it was essential that his wife's disappearance should not even be suspected as a murder. Otherwise he would be suspect No. 1. If she were to disappear, however, without apparently being harmed, she would be listed as a missing person, of which there are hundreds every year. The London area, in the 1970s, recorded about fifty murders a year, a figure that had remained constant since the beginning of the century. But unexplained disappearances are relatively common and most of them remain unexplained. Veronica had been mentally ill. Her fitness to safeguard the children was in question. She was a very isolated person with few people to investigate her mysterious exit. And she had done it before, admittedly for only a few hours, but it was a precedent none the less. If she failed to reappear, then suicide would be the most popular explanation, as indeed it now is in the case of Lucan.

Anyone privy to Lucan's aims in 1974, and making a bet on the outcome, would have concluded that whereas it would be relatively simple for him to murder his wife in an appropriate manner, he would probably fail to spirit away her body. The extraordinary thing is that he failed in the easy task but proved adept at the far more difficult one of arranging the disappearance of his own body at short notice.

In the matter of the murder, the theory goes, Lucan kept things simple. He would kill Veronica at No. 46, the house where he had lived for nine years, which he still visited to see the children and to which he had a key. He would choose the nanny's night off, when his wife would be alone in the house, and a time after the children had gone to bed. He would hit her with a blunt instrument. Discarded lengths of lead piping are not hard to find, thanks to the modern fashion for thin-bore, lightweight copper. He may well have carried out a dress rehearsal on some appropriate object (such as a dead dog or a partially frozen chicken) because the piping was bound in surgical tape. Lucan may have foreseen the severely distorted condition the piping would be in after the attack and may have intended the tape to strengthen it. He would borrow a car with a large boot; he would wear gloves; and he would take with him a suitable sack for the body – a US mailbag.* He would bludgeon his wife to death, place her body and the murder weapon in the mailbag, place the mailbag in the boot of the borrowed car and park the car at some discreet location. He would then return to the Clermont Club, establish his alibi and dispose of the body, preferably before it had even been discovered that his wife was missing. He may have anticipated that the nanny would return home late and go straight to her room, so Veronica's absence would not be detected until the children woke up in the morning.

So much for the murder; Lucan still had to decide on

---

* The mailbag is an unexplained oddity. US mailbags are a rarity in England, and they are not left lying around in the United States either (unlike Post Office bags, which are commonly seen on London's pavements).

how to dispose of the body. The only indication of his plans in this respect, offered by the police, was the discovery of the bloodstained car at the port of Newhaven. Newhaven is the South Coast port closest to London; it has a large boat marina; and a man resembling Lucan was seen in the early hours of the morning after the murder by two fishermen near the small boat pier. Lucan had an expert knowledge of power boats, and it is therefore suggested that he had intended to motor out to sea, drop the weighted sack into very deep water and then return to take custody of his children.

There are, in support of this theory, certain facts which have become known since the police presented their case at the inquest. The writer Taki Theodoracopoulos, a gambling friend of Lucan, has said, without giving the source of the information, that Lucan bought a 20-foot speedboat in the year before he disappeared. Taki says that Lucan kept the boat moored on the South Coast and that during the summer of 1974 he made two dummy runs, in ordinary cars and with a sack weighing 8 stone, from Belgravia to the South Coast. He then transferred the sack from the car to the boat, put out into the Channel and headed for the deepest part. He timed the whole operation and intended to return to the Clermont before midnight on the night of the murder to re-establish his alibi. Taki also said that Lucan borrowed £5,000 from him just before the murder, and that one day he found Lucan training in Hyde Park, which struck him as odd because Lucan had never previously been concerned about his fitness.

It is certainly true that Lucan was an enthusiast for power boats; he had competed in the Cowes–Torquay race, and at the time he became engaged to Veronica he talked about power boats incessantly. Furthermore, he knew a lot about the Channel, both the sea and the coast. Some years earlier, when he was younger, his friend the late 'Pips' Royston had fallen in love with the daughter of the Comte de Paris, pretender to the throne of France. Viscount Royston's suit was not welcomed by the Comte, so Royston decided that he would have to abduct the object of his passion. He did not abduct her but he got as far as planning the operation, relying for technical advice on his friend John Bingham, who proved highly knowledgeable about clandestine routes between France and England, reliable fishermen, suitable beaches, tidal patterns and so on.

For Lucan the Channel was the ideal oubliette. It had been his happy hunting ground. Now it would be the place where everything would, once again, start to come right. The weighted sack would sink into the grey waters above Seven-Mile Bottom, and for Lucan at least the sun would start to shine. As Veronica disappeared into the darkness he would, in the words of Ben Hecht, 'make a little holiday in his heart'.

But, dammit, it did not work out like that. None of Lucan's plans could account for the disappearance of *two* women. With Mrs Rivett dead and his wife running screaming out of the house, there was little left for him to do. He himself disappeared into the night. His movements can, almost, be accounted for. The time was 9.45 p.m. Apparently covered in blood, he left the house by the front door, closing it behind him, got into the borrowed car and drove away, avoiding his flat. Instead he drove round to Chester Square and stopped at the house of a friend, Madeleine Floorman. He rang her doorbell for a very long time. He was in a state of shock. Mrs Floorman says that she was alone in the house and did not respond. Later, stains (apparently blood stains, though they were never submitted for police examination) were found on the doorstep. Shortly after the doorbell stopped ringing, the telephone rang. Mrs Floorman was certain the call did not come from a call box. Lucan did not identify himself but she recognized his voice. His remarks were incoherent. Then he rang off. Lucan also telephoned his mother, again not from a call box, sufficiently soon for her to arrive at Lower Belgrave Street by about 10.45. He then drove to Uckfield, to the house of his friends the Maxwell-Scotts, where he arrived some time after 11 p.m. He left that house at about 1.15 and was never seen again.

The only other signs of life from Lucan were three letters and one telephone call. In his conversation with Mrs Maxwell-Scott he rehearsed the story he was to tell his mother. He said that while passing the house he had seen a fight in the basement, that he had gone in and slipped in a pool of blood, and that the man, a large man, had made off. Lucan then wrote two letters to Bill Shand Kydd, put them in separate envelopes and asked Mrs Maxwell-Scott to post them. He had a second telephone conversation with his mother at 12.15, establishing that the children were safe and saying that he would call the police in the morning. He refused Mrs Maxwell-Scott's offer of a bed for the night and drove away in a 'dark saloon', at about 1.15. No one has admitted to seeing him since. At some time he wrote a third letter to Michael Stoop and omitted to stamp it. Mr Stoop destroyed the envelope so it is not known when or where this was posted. Mr Stoop told the police that he thought it had been written on notepaper that he kept in the glove pocket of the car he lent to Lucan.

The Ford Corsair was found in Newhaven on Sunday, 10 November. It was parked at some distance from the sea front. It is thought to have been left there between 5 and 8 o'clock on the Friday morning – that is, between four and seven hours after Lucan left Mrs Maxwell-Scott. The general view was that Lucan had taken his speedboat out into the Channel, lashed himself on, opened the water cocks and gone down with his ship.

CHAPTER FOUR

Honour, Privilege, Action

If I had to choose between betraying my country and
betraying my friends, I hope I should have the guts to
betray my country.

E. M. Forster, 'What I Believe'

It would be fair to say that in conducting their initial
investigation at No. 46 the officers of Gerald Road police
station did not rush in mob-handed. The last time they had
been faced with such a delicate problem had been in 1946,
when there was a murder at 45 Chester Square, the wartime
home of King George of Greece. On that occasion the
housekeeper had been shot in the 'ground-floor back.'
Now, less than thirty years later, the nobs were at it again.
In the Lucan case the police were immediately confronted
by the Dowager Countess, who gave them the story of her
son's marriage from a mother's point of view.* This appar-

---

* Detective Sergeant Forsyth said that when Lord Lucan's mother arrived at
  No. 46, she told him that Veronica was being treated for her 'mental complaint' and that she was a manic-depressive who had been described in court
  as 'dangerous to the children'.

ently caused them to hesitate before drawing the obvious conclusions. By 6 o'clock on the morning following the murder the police had obtained a statement from Lady Lucan in which she accused her husband of murdering Sandra Rivett and of trying to murder her. By midday it must have become clear that Lord Lucan was not going to contact the police as he had said he would. And yet no move was made to obtain a warrant for his arrest until the following Tuesday. Without a warrant, attempts to track Lord Lucan were severely hampered. Searches of private property could not be carried out. A message was immediately flashed to Interpol, but since it read, 'Richard John Bingham, Earl of Lucan, wanted for murder and attempted murder. Please arrest. Extradition will follow,' the average South American immigration officer may reasonably have failed to deduce that he was meant to be looking for either John Lucan or Lord Lucan.

There was, of course, another ground for hesitation. Under English law a wife may not give evidence against her husband except in the case of crimes committed against herself. Veronica could not have been called as a witness in the trial of Lucan for the murder of Sandra Rivett. None the less, a warrant does not have to lead to a trial. It can be based on no more than reasonable grounds for suspicion. It is still not entirely clear why the police did not obtain a warrant for Lucan's arrest until the Tuesday. By then it was becoming obvious to Detective Chief Superintendent Ranson that his inquiries would not be straightforward for entirely different reasons.

On the Friday morning Mrs Maxwell-Scott stamped the letters to Bill Shand Kydd and posted them. The midday papers carried the first news of events in Lower Belgrave Street, and the fact that police wanted to interview Lord Lucan, but Mrs Maxwell-Scott did not contact the police. Asked subsequently why she had not done so, she replied:

'I had no reason to.' Meanwhile in London Mr Ranson received no telephone call from Lucan, but he did receive numerous other calls, all misleading and anonymous, reporting that Lucan had been seen in London. Later Mr Ranson, rather charitably, put these calls down to the 'horseplay of the upper classes'.

On that Friday too John Aspinall invited several of Lucan's friends to lunch. Those present included Stephen Raphael, Lucan's stockbroker and gambling mentor; Bill Shand Kydd; Daniel Meinertzhagen, a banker; Charles Benson, the racing correspondent of the *Daily Express*; and Dominick Elwes. All over London, Lucan's friends had begun to rally round. Their telephones were off the hook; no one was to be available until a plan had been formed. Aspinall said of the lunch, 'People were worried about what to do if he turned up. He might have turned up at Howletts [Aspinall's house], he might have telephoned from Brazil, so every contingency was looked at.' Various schemes for assisting Lucan were discussed, some of them, according to Charles Benson, 'more melodramatic and ludicrous than others'. Not everyone was equally concerned about the fate of their friend. Some were more worried about being placed in the same situation as Mrs Maxwell-Scott. At least one of Lucan's friends telephoned from abroad and told his factotum that if Lucan turned up at the house, he was to be turned away at the door. One positive step was taken at the lunch. It was agreed that someone should try to find out what Veronica had told the police. Dominick Elwes, as the nicest person present, was chosen for this task and dispatched to St George's Hospital carrying a large bunch of flowers. He was accompanied by Hugh Bingham, Lucan's brother. They were eventually admitted to Veronica's room, which was under police guard, and when Veronica told them that Lucan had tried to kill her, Elwes, overcome by the tragedy and the sight of Veronica's wounds, burst into tears. Veronica Lucan, who knew exactly why he had come, was not particularly impressed, but, unusually among Lucan's friends, Elwes was certain of Lucan's guilt from then on.

Most of the others, convinced of Lucan's innocence, closed ranks. Aspinall spoke for them all when he said, 'If a close friend of yours came in covered in blood, having done some frightful deed, the last thing that would have occurred to you is to turn him in. It goes against every last instinct of human loyalties, and to hell with the law or the common norms of civic behaviour or something. If he had begged asylum, he would have had it. I would have helped him . . . If he had turned up at Howletts, I would have taken him aside and had a long talk and looked at the problem. It may have involved him giving himself up or getting him funds to go to Costa Rica. He could certainly have had a lot of money. I had many people calling me and saying, if Lucan wants money, he can have it.' Aspinall, then, was the self-appointed staff officer for the great escape. In his unmistakably contemptuous tones one can catch the authentic, confident echo of privilege, the love of adventure, the sense of himself and his friends as a bunch of outlaws, the sense of lawlessness. It was the triumphant reassertion of a neglected point of view, a reminder that behind the prevailing ethos, property and all it entailed was biding its time. 'If the law doesn't suit, then change it. If you can't change it, damn the law.'

On the Saturday morning the police were told of the bloodstained letters that had reached Mr Shand Kydd. Mr Ranson was interested by the Uckfield postmarks, and when he asked Shand Kydd about the possibility of Lucan's having a friend in Uckfield he learnt of the Maxwell-Scotts. In due course he obtained a statement from Mrs Maxwell-Scott. All this time, of course, someone else, the person who provided Lucan with a telephone for his first and second calls, was saying nothing about it.

Other people continued to offer the police anonymous and misleading information. The police had found Lucan's three address books in his flat and had started to work their way through the list of names. It was one of Lucan's more eccentric habits that he should have chosen to compile these books, which are thought to have contained the names and addresses of almost everyone he had ever met. People who had encountered him only once, sometimes years before, were astonished to be approached by the police. As the inquiry continued and word got around, the police methods began to amuse Lucan's friends. The relationships between those charged with investigating the murder of Sandra Rivett and those who 'knew nothing about it' continued to deteriorate. Lady Amabel Lindsay, 'Pips' Royston's sister, whose husband Patrick, a director of Christie's, was to be responsible for the sale of Lucan's silver, was delighted when she asked one policeman, 'What do *you* think happened?', and drew the guarded response, 'We're not paid to think, madam.' The most notorious comment, which must have been intended to shock, was: 'Such a pity. Nannies are so hard to find nowadays.'

Mr Ranson, who started his work politely and with the assumption that those who had nothing to hide would be anxious to help, found himself, as he put it, coming up against 'the attitude of some of these people, trying to put one over us, to take us on and beat us'. The matter became sufficiently well known to be raised in Parliament by a Labour MP, Marcus Lipton, who suggested that the police were not getting full co-operation and that some people were being 'a bit snooty'. Charles Benson, on behalf of Lucan's friends, replied to this suggestion at once in a letter to *The Times*. 'As far as I know,' he wrote, 'all [Lord Lucan's] friends have made themselves available to the police at all times. I personally rang the department con-

cerned on the Friday morning following the murder.' Mr
Benson, of course, unlike Mrs Maxwell-Scott, knew
nothing of Lucan's movements after he left Belgravia.
During the weeks after the murder the police undertook
the fairly hopeless task of searching several of the stately
houses of England. Holkham Hall, the Earl of Leicester's
seat, was visited, as was Warwick Castle, which belonged
to Lucan's cousin, the Earl of Warwick.

When the police reached Howletts, John Aspinall's
house, tempers began to fray. At the time rumours were
circulating that Lucan had committed suicide and that
Aspinall had disposed of his body by feeding it to the
tigers in his celebrated private zoo. Aspinall's tigers were
known to be partial to human flesh, following several
unfortunate accidents, and, in James Fox's words, the
'conventional wisdom' was that 'Aspinall's tigers eat the
bones as well.' By the time they reached Howletts the
police were frustrated and irritated. They were not amused
when Aspinall asked them if they wanted to lift all the
floorboards. They asked him if he was proud to be the
friend of a man who had tried to bash his wife to death.
Aspinall replied, by his own account, with a typically florid
outburst: 'I said, if she'd been my wife, I'd have bashed
her to death five years before and so would you. I said,
don't come that line with me because who knows into
what red hell one's sightly soul will stray under the pressure
of a long, dripping attrition of a woman who's always out
to reduce you, to whom you are stuck and from whom
you've had children.' Sometimes Aspinall in full flow
sounds like a violent version of Mr Micawber.

But the police search did turn up one important piece of
additional evidence. On 14 November, one week after the
murder, Greville Howard, who lived at 5 Eaton Row, the
mews house at the back of 46 Lower Belgrave Street, and
who had been among those who had waited for Lucan at

the Clermont Club on the previous Thursday night, went to Gerald Road police station. (Lady Lucan had returned home from hospital the day before.) While he was being questioned the police let themselves into the house and searched it. Later they said that Mr Howard had gone to the police station 'of his own accord'. Months later, at the inquest, it was revealed that Howard had made a statement to the police in which he said that a fortnight before the murder – that is, at about the time Lucan borrowed Michael Stoop's car – he had had a conversation with Lord Lucan. During the conversation Lucan had complained about his money problems, and Howard had advised him to go bankrupt. Lucan had said, 'There's another way out – to kill Veronica.' Howard had said, 'Don't be absurd,' and had pointed out that the children might have been upset by such a course of action. Lucan had then developed his plan. He mentioned dumping Veronica's body in the Solent, and pointed out that he would then be able to sell the house in Lower Belgrave Street. That much information was leaked after the inquest, although the evidence was never tested under cross-examination because Howard fell ill at that time.*

Normally the death of Sandra Rivett would have been followed a week or so later by an inquest, but on this occasion the hearing was postponed to enable the police to make an arrest. Once someone was charged with murder,

---

* One of the police officers on the case was interested enough, during the inquest, to visit the private hospital where Howard was undergoing treatment for a bad back, the Nuffield in Babington. He spoke to one of the nurses on the floor. Howard's statement against Lucan was the only example of one of the 'Eton mafia' (as they were known in Gerald Road) speaking against the fugitive. But, in view of Howard's failure to come to court, it can have given the police little confidence that they had at last received the full-hearted co-operation they needed. The police got the impression that the others thought Howard had made a mistake.

the inquest would become a formality and the manner of her death could be thoroughly investigated at a criminal trial. In the months of waiting, during which no arrest was made, a parallel investigation began to unfold. The police wanted Lord Lucan, but a number of other people were more interested in his money. In his second letter to Bill Shand Kydd, headed 'Financial Matters', Lucan had listed the items of silver which were to be sold at Christie's and had asked Shand Kydd to agree the reserve prices he had estimated. At the end of the list Lucan had written, 'Proceeds to go to Lloyds, Coutts and National Westminster – and the other creditors can get lost for the time being.' As we have seen, Lucan's overdrafts (he also had one at the Midland Bank) totalled £14,177 at this time. The sale of silver went ahead on 27 November and the lots, listed as 'the property of a nobleman', raised £17,410. Because the Midland Bank had been omitted from the prepared list of creditors, one of Lucan's gambling friends, Jimmy Goldsmith, had to stump up £5,000 for the Midland loan which he had guaranteed.

Other creditors were less fortunate. On 28 January 1975 two of them, H.W. Motors Ltd and Bowater Securities, moved to have Lucan declared bankrupt. They were owed £1,500 for the Lucan Mercedes and in their petition claimed that Lucan 'with intent to defeat or delay his creditors departed out of England on or about 8 November 1974'. A trustee in bankruptcy was appointed, and Lucan was found to have debts of £58,901. These included debts to Harrods for cigars and wine, to Cartier's for a crocodile-skin watch strap and to a gunsmith's for repairs to his shotguns. £11,800 was owed for unpaid gambling chips. And there were the usual bills for rent, gas and electricity, both for his flat in Elizabeth Street and for No. 46.

During the course of the next eighteen months the trustee, Dennis Gilson, a certified accountant with an office in Islington, found himself in the unusual position of having legally privileged access to the personal affairs of the fugitive in a murder hunt. Mr Gilson discovered that Lord Lucan had a bank account in Switzerland and another in Rhodesia. He asked the Foreign Office and the Bank of England to request the Swiss government to allow him access to the Berne account, but the request was only granted, for the second time in Swiss banking history, following the intervention of an international bank. Mr Gilson went through Lucan's belongings. He opened the black tin trunk where Lucan's coronet and ermine coronation robes were kept, wrapped in tissue paper, for his annual visit to the House of Lords to attend the State Opening of Parliament. The robes and coronet were sold, as was the rest of the silver, some of it fetching record prices in Geneva. Also auctioned was an octagonal gold watch inscribed 'Lucky, God bless yer'. It fetched £1,000. The robes had been made for his grandfather, the 5th Earl, and would in normal circumstances have been passed on to Lucan's son. But once a trustee in bankruptcy has been appointed his decision is final until the bankrupt is discharged. It was an extraordinary feature of the Lucan case that two British legal procedures which are infrequent enough to be relatively unpredictable – the inquest on murder and the proceedings in bankruptcy – should both have come into play. In the event Mr Gilson was able to repay all Lucan's creditors in full. Because of the interest, fees, legal costs, tax and expenses involved, he eventually had to raise £118,000 from the estate. It turned out that the lease of No. 46 could not be sold because it was owned not by Lucan but by the family trust. None of the furnishings at No. 46 had to be taken. The £15,000 in the Bulawayo bank account remained undisturbed because it had been blocked as a result of the sanctions then in force against Rhodesia. The £3,000 borrowed at the ex-

The 3rd Earl of Lucan (1800–1888), who ordered the Charge of the Light Brigade in 1854. He lived to be the oldest soldier in the British Army.

The 7th Earl of Cardigan (1797–1868), who led the Light Brigade at Balaclava. He was Lord Lucan's brother-in-law and could not stand the sight of him.

The Charge of the Light Cavalry Brigade, 25 October 1854: a drawing by W. Simpson.

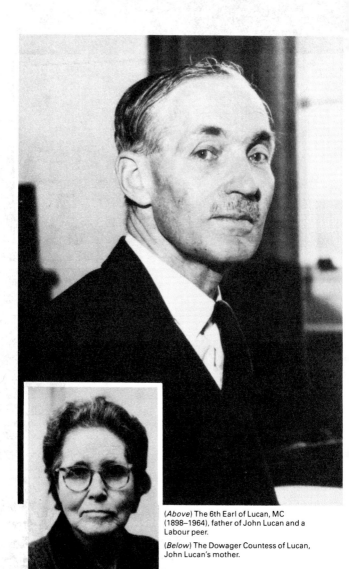

(*Above*) The 6th Earl of Lucan, MC (1898–1964), father of John Lucan and a Labour peer.

(*Below*) The Dowager Countess of Lucan, John Lucan's mother.

Above) John Bingham at the helm of the *Migrant*, 15 August 1964, off Cowes, Isle of Wight, at the start of the International Offshore Powerboat Race.

Below) John Bingham in October 1963: an engagement picture.

Lord Lucan in his ceremonial robes.

(*Opposite*) John and Veronica Lucan on their wedding day, 28 November 1963.

(*Above*) A rare photograph of Lord Lucan playing bridge.

(*Above, opposite*) Lady Lucan with her sister Christina Shand Kydd.
(*Below, opposite*) John Lucan and Dominick Elwes on holiday in Acapulco in March 1973.

Sandra Rivett, nanny to the Lucan children, in November 1974.

orbitant rate of interest was in the first place repaid by the guarantor, another of Lucan's friends, 'Mr Parkes'.

As the weeks passed and there was no sign of Lord Lucan, it became clear that a date for the inquest would have to be set. The prevailing opinion was that Lucan had been driven to desperate measures by an impossible wife, since this was the view of the only people around who knew the family background, but meanwhile a third investigator was at work whose activities were ultimately to have fatal consequences.

James Fox, like many of those involved in the story, had been to school at Eton and he had found it easier than most reporters to gain access to the 'Clermont set'. He was preparing a long article for the *Sunday Times Magazine* and received the particular help of two of Lucan's friends, John Aspinall and Dominick Elwes. Although Fox was an Old Etonian, his political views were somewhat to the left of those who haunted the Clermont Club, and his article, when it eventually appeared, disappointed the friends of Lord Lucan, who had supposed that the piece would be sympathetic to him. Fox had become intrigued by the isolation and exaggerated dislike that afflicted Veronica Lucan. His piece was required reading for anyone interested in the story. It appeared the week before the inquest opened, and it changed the climate of public opinion. The consequences of this destabilizing intervention in a family crisis that was already far advanced were to be far more drastic than anyone could have foreseen. Inhibited by the pending hearing, the newspapers had reported very little of the dispute and the rather callous attitude of the 'Clermont set' to the fate of Sandra Rivett. Lucan's friends had, until the publication of Fox's article, had it all their own way. They had been able both to blacken Veronica's name and to conceal their less attractive features. With the opening of the inquest they lost control of the plot, and the family privacy, which they prized so highly, was well and truly breached.

In order to understand the extraordinary nature of the inquest into the death of Sandra Rivett it is necessary to grasp that Lucan's family and friends, however chilling their attitudes may have appeared, were sincere in their opinions. They did value personal honour greatly; they saw nothing reprehensible in taking their privileges for granted and using them to the full; they considered themselves to be an embattled group, cut off in a hostile world, who had the moral right to take all necessary steps to ensure their own survival. Honour, privilege, action: these were the mainsprings of life as they intended to lead it. They failed, of course – everyone fails to achieve the ideal – but they were usually allowed to fail in private. The inquest put an end to that. On that professional stage they were made to appear selfish, heartless, antediluvian, dangerously close to being unworthy of respect, dangerously close to being ridiculous. And yet they were not alone in their conception of how they were expected to behave. Indeed, there was about the reporting of the inquest a strong sense of people playing out their ancient roles.

During the hearing Albert and Eunice Hensby, the parents of Sandra Rivett, sat at the back of the court, generally ignored. Mr Hensby, a factory worker, said: 'My daughter's name has hardly been mentioned. Yet she is the reason why we are all here.' And Sandra's aunt, Mrs Vera Ward, said: 'Sandra is in what seems to be a battle between two sides of the Lucan family.' Sandra's sister, Charmaine, said: 'Because of the Lucan family's squabble no one seems to spare a thought for poor Sandra.' Albert, Vera and Charmaine were mourning the death of Sandra. They did not have to suffer from an inflated view of their own importance to expect that a public inquest into such a terrible event would bestow its own importance, the last public importance, on the person who had died. Yet they

did not apparently consid_____
important as the Lucans. _____
invited people to overlook the__
family were hurt that Lady Luca_____
letter of sympathy. And she comp_____
Ward had called to collect Sandra's_____
bundled in a paper bag and Lady Lucan _____ver
at the door.' The Hensbys expected of La_____ certain
standards which would be applied even in di___ult circumstances. They expected tact and consideration. They did
not expect paper parcels to be handed over at the door.

At the same time, the fact that the man sought for the
murder of Sandra Rivett was so 'important', in a way that
was conventionally denied, added a dimension to her end.
If she had been killed by the milkman, there would have
been no reporters in court for Mr and Mrs Hensby to
complain to. The English fascination with the English
upper class continues. The actor Gerald Harper, who
played a strong-featured aristo in a popular television
series, said that the reason for the popularity of the series
lay in just one line of the script, frequently repeated, 'Thank
you, Sutton' – words that every Englishman yearns to say
to his butler. Harper prepared carefully for his part, and at
one point he even played golf with a real nobleman, Lord
Lucan. Later he said that he had noticed how Lucan, a
perfectly affable figure, treated his caddy. Whereas Harper
was on first-name terms by the second hole, Lucan treated
his man throughout the round as though he wasn't there.
On another occasion, shooting, Harper remembered an
incident when one of the upper-class infants patted a
gundog, which promptly bit him. The owner of the
child then rushed up to apologize to the owner of the *dog*.
It was the unconsciously humorous character of this
world, Lucan's world, that came vividly to life at the
inquest. It was almost as though another television series,

nstairs, had been reshot by Alfred Hitchcock.
quired no special effort by the Lucan family witnesses for this illusion to be created. There was, for instance, the wonderfully archaic use of language. The
Dowager Countess of Lucan, a veteran socialist politician,
who, according to one of Lucan's friends, had been 'trained
in Moscow', describing her son's second telephone call on
the night of the murder said: 'He sounded more on all
fours.' By this phrase she intended to convey that a grown
man was at last behaving normally. Later she said that her
son had told her he had 'spotted' a struggle through the
basement window but that the man attacking Veronica had
'made off'.

In a letter describing the conversation he had with
Veronica after she was attacked Lucan said, 'She lay doggo
for a bit.' And 'I will lie doggo,' he wrote. Describing
Veronica's feelings, Lucan wrote, 'She has demonstrated
her hatred for me in the past.' The Dowager said that
when she told Christina that her sister was in hospital,
Christina said, 'Has she attempted to kill herself again?'
The stilted, correct syntax was infectious. One observer
said of Lady Lucan that she was 'fearful of incurring her
husband's displeasure'. Counsel for the Dowager argued
against a verdict that would be 'bound to bring stigma' to
the family name. Lucan again, in his letter to Michael
Stoop describing the most terrible event in his life, wrote,
'I won't bore you with anything or involve you . . .' Stoop
himself, when asked why Lucan had asked to borrow
his inconspicuous Ford rather than the Mercedes, replied:
'I imagine through natural good manners he did not want
to deprive me of my better car.' The note of cold rebuke
rang clear. So much for a murder plot. Even the wit
emerged in this stilted form. When questioned by reporters
after the verdict, the Dowager replied, 'I do not think this
is serving any useful purpose. No comment. It is a useful

phrase and I shall have a rec
of the portable tape-recorder
escaped her attention.

When people become evasive,
refuge in an irrelevant sincerity. If
they hope to do so with convincing
consideration, form: there was nothing ass   ing-
hams' emphasis on these. If they sometim   ided like
characters from a play by Noël Coward, that was because
the playwright had modelled his dialogue on theirs.

The strain in Lucan's character which may have led him
to 'take matters into his own hands', 'not to take the loss
of his children lying down', was partly lawless, partly based
on a belief in privilege and partly a reflection of his sense
of responsibility for his children. Anyone who decides to
kill to redress a wrong has taken a decision in favour of
action in its most extreme form. Such action has to be its
own justification; the world will be changed, whether for
better or worse, and the man who chooses to act has no
right to complain of the consequences. He must simply
accept them, foreseen or not. If you outrage the 'civic
norm', the rules of decency, morality, consideration, you
are beyond the possibility of complaint. You are committed
to the action, wherever it takes you.

In the case of Lucan, his belief in action, shared by his
friends, extended to politics. There was occasional talk of
going into exile, fleeing the revolution, ways of escape,
keeping one's wealth portable. Elwes had links with Colonel
David Stirling, who had commanded the SAS. In 1974
Michael Stoop, the gambler, volunteered to join the army
of vigilantes recruited by Colonel Stirling in the face of
trade-union militancy with a view to 'keeping the country
going'. Greville Howard read the speeches of Enoch
Powell and thoroughly approved of them. He wrote to
congratulate Mr Powell on his views on immigration policy

...quently undertook research work at Powell's
..., acting as his political secretary. This was a high-
status position in the world of the Clermont Club; it was
within snapping distance of the red meat of power. Lucan
spoke, approvingly, of hanging and flogging and, dis-
approvingly, of 'niggers'. In the evening, over dinner,
the concerned members of the Clermont plotted a military
coup; next morning they settled for a round of golf with
an invisible caddy. They held forth on the world, often at
great length, not always very interestingly, frequently to
their wives. In December 1973, in the Muthaiga Club in
Kenya where Lucan had once been a frequent visitor, one
such conversation went as follows:

He: They call strikes 'industrial action' now. God.
(*Pause.*) We're so decadent in Britain. What we
need is good old-fashioned Fascism.

She: Enoch Powell, dear, not Fascism.

He: Enoch Powell and the Fourth Reich! To get rid
of the communists and anarchists and subver-
sives.

She: I see they're locking the platform gates now to
prevent the commuters beating up the train
drivers. Well, I hope they break the gates down
and beat them up anyway. (*Helps herself to salad.*)

He: (*Irritably*) But that sort of violence is not the
province of the individual. It is the province of
the state. The state must be the ultimate brutality!

She: Salad, dear?

Later the discussion moved to servants.

She: You have no idea how dirty everything is, and
how dirty they are. They are filthy.

He: But I don't mind how bad at it they are. I want a
servant. I want to be *served*.

They were frightened people. They watched the Portuguese revolution on their television screens, the political policemen being lynched, the Portuguese peasants being urged to form co-operatives and seize land owned by English expatriates without compensation. It was the end of one of the three remaining right-wing dictatorships in Europe. In Spain Franco was being kept alive by machines. In Uganda an English teacher, formerly an officer in the British Army, had become the plaything of an insubordinate African buffoon. Brigadier Frank Kitson, fresh from his tour of duty in Northern Ireland, had published *Low Intensity Operations*, which described a military response to urban terrorism. On the whole, those in the Clermont Club did not take the rosy view. It was a time when playing God had extra attractions. For the political analysts of the house without a clock it was all too easy to lose their sense of time and place. The lynch mobs of Lisbon, hunting down Salazar's secret police, could be heard baying distantly from the upper floors of Berkeley Square. The election of a Labour government was a 'pre-revolutionary situation'; money had to be made fast; no holds were barred; the weakest – including the weakest inside the Clermont Club – would go to the wall. Such was the average grasp of reality that someone like Lucan's mother, the kindly, dry, thoughtful Dowager, secretary of the mild St Marylebone Labour Party, was 'to all intents and purposes a communist', 'trained in Moscow'; she was regarded as a personal tragedy for her son and for the family honour, on a par with Balaclava. When Lucan disappeared into the night these were the people who felt they should ring Aspinall and offer to help. A year after he had gone some of Lucan's friends were still on the *qui vive*. Lord Suffolk, meeting John Mortimer at a house party in France, felt obliged to inquire whether there was any time limit on murder charges in English law.

CHAPTER FIVE

The Trial of
Lord Lucan

Audi Alteram Partem – No man should be condemned
unheard.

From *The Principles of Natural Justice*

And so, more than seven months after Sandra Rivett's
death, the inquest opened at Westminster Coroner's Court,
on Monday, 16 June 1975. The coroner, Dr Gavin
Thurston, started by explaining to the jury the unusual
circumstances of this inquest. He said that if someone was
charged before justices, the coroner did not enter the
picture. If there was a murder followed by a suicide, the
jury would return the appropriate verdicts. If there was a
murder for which no one was traced, then the correct
verdict would be murder by person or persons unknown.
Finally, there was an excessively rare case in which a
coroner's court still had the power, if it found a person
responsible for a murder, to commit that person to trial at
the Crown Court. Dr Thurston said that he had delayed
the inquest for a long time in the hope that something

more concrete would turn up. And he had decided to call the first witness, Lady Lucan, only 'after a great deal of very anxious consideration'. He then invited Lady Lucan to give an account of events in her house on that night.

When she had completed her evidence Lady Lucan was questioned by Mr Brian Watling, who represented the police. He wished her to embellish her account of the fight between herself and her husband, perhaps thinking that the jury might wonder how she had managed to survive it. Lady Lucan had originally said that somehow or other she got between her husband's legs on the ground and that her husband then desisted in his attempts to strangle her and gouge out her eye. Mr Watling said, 'When you were struggling with your husband, it is right you grabbed hold of him?' Lady Lucan agreed. 'By his private parts?' 'Yes.' She added that the effect of this was to make her husband step back. Lord Lucan had apparently said something at this stage, but the coroner would not allow Lady Lucan to say what it was. She had, in fact, told the police that she had said, 'Where's Sandra?' and Lucan had replied, 'She's out.' Later he had admitted that Sandra was dead, that her body was in the basement and that his wife must not go and look as it was such a mess. But the jury heard none of this.

The direction that proceedings were to take became apparent immediately after Mr Watling sat down and Michael Eastham, QC, began to cross-examine Lady Lucan. He told the jury that he appeared for Lord Lucan's mother and that he was looking after the Earl's interests because the jury might reach a decision which would be 'bound to bring stigma' to his name. He added that this involved 'the inescapable and unpleasant duty of suggesting that what Lady Lucan is saying she knows to be untrue'. His first question was: 'Even before your separation you entertained feelings of hatred against your

husband, did you not?' There were immediate objections
and the coroner said that it was a very strong way of
putting it. Mr Eastham then read out the first letter from
Lucan to Bill Shand Kydd in which Lucan said that he had
seen an intruder, that he had interrupted a fight and that
his wife had accused him of hiring the murderer. 'Veronica
will say it was all my doing . . .,' the letter continued.
'Veronica has demonstrated her hatred for me in the past
and will do anything to see me accused.' The letter ended
with the words: 'When they [the children] are old enough
to understand explain to them the dream of paranoia and
look after them.' Mr Eastham said that these words would
be totally inexplicable to the jury without further evidence.
In reply Mr Bryan Coles, for Lady Lucan, pointed out that
the proceedings between the Lucans in the Family Division
had been held *in camera*. The jury were then sent out for
fifteen minutes while the ground rules for the cross-
examination were disputed. From then on it was an uphill
struggle for Mr Eastham. When the jury returned he said to
the coroner, 'In view of the ruling you have given in the
absence of the jury, I do not think I can assist the jury at all
and I do not wish to ask the lady any questions.' Mr
Eastham had intended to establish that because of Lady
Lucan's hatred for Lord Lucan she was inventing a story
to his discredit and that therefore it would be unsafe for
the jury to conclude that Lucan had attacked and killed
Sandra Rivett. This was a hopeless task in a coroner's
court which by tradition forbids questions to the general
discredit of a witness.

Lady Lucan was in the witness box for two hours, her
head and shoulders just visible above the wooden rim. On
that first day, as on all successive days, she wore the same
outfit of black velvet coat and white turban hat which
helped to conceal her head wounds. This repeated choice
of costume gave an accurate impression of poverty. After

completing her evidence she returned to the bench in the court, where she sat alone, but for her police guard, directly behind her mother-in-law and her sister. James Fox noticed that the huge ruby clasp which fastened Christina's pearls was therefore, for much of the time, directly in front of Veronica's face.

Further evidence given on the first day included a statement, which was read out by the policewoman who had taken it, from the 10-year-old Lady Frances Bingham and evidence both from the two policemen who had found Sandra Rivett's body and from the police surgeon who had certified death, Dr Michael Smith; he said that, in his opinion, death had taken place 'only shortly before the body was discovered'. Finally, counsel for Sandra Rivett's family asked whether the weapon that had wounded Lady Lucan had resembled the weapon that had killed Sandra Rivett and was told that it had.

On the second day of the hearing a senior Home Office pathologist, Dr Keith Simpson, who carried out the post-mortem, apparently disagreed with the police surgeon about the time of death. He thought that death had taken place within a minute or two of the attack and before her body had been doubled up and placed in the bag.

He was followed by a series of witnesses who attempted to put Lord Lucan's side of events. The first of these was Lucan's mother, the Dowager Lady Lucan, then 75 years old. Despite her age she declined to sit down. She affirmed – the oath of an atheist – and started her account by saying that she disagreed with the police estimate of the time of the first telephone call from her son. The police put the time at 10.25; she thought it was about 10 p.m. There were no call-box pips. She said John had told her that there had been a terrible catastrophe at No. 46. Veronica was hurt; the nanny was badly hurt; he wanted her to collect the children as quickly as possible and ring Bill Shand Kydd for help. She said that was the whole of the conversation, although Detective Sergeant Graham Forsyth, who had become Lady Lucan's bodyguard, had earlier said that when the Dowager reached the house at about 10.45 p.m. she informed him that her son had told her he was driving past the house, saw a fight going on in the basement between a man and Veronica and went in; that Veronica was shouting and screaming; and that her son sounded very shocked.

Later that night, 'well after midnight', after she had returned to her own house with the children, she received another telephone call. It was her son. She asked him where he was but was apparently not told. He asked her about the children and was assured that they were asleep. He asked about Veronica, and his mother said that she was in hospital. She then said, 'Look, the police are here. Do you want to speak to them?' On replacing the receiver she said to the police constable, 'That was my son. He won't speak to you now. He will phone you in the morning.'

Mr Brian Watling asked the Dowager about a number of inconsistencies in the evidence compared with the statement she had made to the police. Had Lord Lucan said that he had 'interrupted' a fight in the basement or 'seen' one? She replied that she had a 'subjective impression' that he had said 'interrupted' but that she thought the upshot of both statements was the same. Mr Watling then asked whether she had contacted Mrs Shand Kydd and told her that her sister was in hospital. The Dowager Countess said she had and that Christina had replied, 'Has she attempted to kill herself again?' This reply caused a noticeable feeling of shock among those in court.

Mr Watling concluded by saying, 'I don't think that I'll take this any further. The jury has seen this lady for themselves.' Mr Eastham, the Dowager's counsel, protested that this was a most improper remark and he strongly objected to it. The coroner asked that the press should not print the remark, but it was reported anyway.

In addition, the Dowager Countess told the coroner that she used to see her son about once every ten days; that his feelings for his children were strong and passionate – 'more like an obsession'; that it came as a great disappointment to him that he did not have custody of them; that she knew very little about her son's income except that he was extremely generous; and that shortly before November she had lent her son £4,000 towards the costs of the custody proceedings.

She said that the word 'upset' was not strong enough to describe her son's voice during the first telephone conversation. He had muttered quite a bit, using words like 'blood' and 'mess'. They were not part of a coherent statement but expressions of horror and disgust. She said that she very much regretted that she had not pressed the point when her son hesitated before declining to speak to the police.

The rest of the proceedings on the second day were dominated by the evidence of Susan Maxwell-Scott. Mrs Maxwell-Scott said that Lucan had arrived at her house in Uckfield at about 11.30 that night. She said that she and her husband had been friends of Lord Lucan for a long time. 'He was always a first friend of my husband,' she said. When he arrived he had not been hysterical but he had been shocked. She had given him a Scotch and water. He looked dishevelled whereas he normally looked very tidy. He had a wet patch on the right hip of his trousers. He spoke of an 'unbelievable nightmare experience', so extraordinary no one would believe it. He said that he had been walking past the house on his way to change for dinner.

'The word "walking" is rather important,' interrupted the coroner.

'Yes,' said Mrs Maxwell-Scott, 'I am almost certain he

used the word. He could have said "passing" and I assumed he was walking. He told me that, on looking through the venetian blind in the basement, he saw a man attacking his wife, so he let himself in with his door key and went down to the basement. As he entered the hall he slipped in a pool of blood. He was not telling this like a story. It came out in bits and this is my best attempt to tell you what he said to me. The man he had seen attacking his wife ran off. Whether this was on hearing Lucan coming down the stairs or whether it was on seeing him, I am not clear. Lucan said the man made off. Lucan, perhaps unfortunately, refrained from chasing the man but went to his wife.'

> *The coroner*: He did not say where the man ran off?
> *A*: No. He said the man made off. Perhaps through the back door, I don't know.
> *Q*: He went to his wife?
> *A*: Yes. She was covered in blood and very hysterical.
> *Q*: Did he say anything further about what his wife said?
> *A*: Yes. He said first she was very hysterical and cried out to him that someone had killed Sandra, then almost in the same breath accused Lucan of having hired the man to kill her. This was something she frequently accused him of – a contract to kill. Lucan claimed it came from an American TV movie.

Lucan, continued Mrs Maxwell-Scott, told her he tried to calm his wife. He took her upstairs. It was his intention to get some towels to mop up the blood and see how bad it was, then to telephone the doctor and the police. He said he felt 'rather squeamish with the blood'. He went to the bathroom and starting soaking the towels, but while he was there Lady Lucan left the bedroom, ran down the stairs and out of the house. Lucan then left the house himself and telephoned his mother and asked her to look after the children. After telling this story Lucan telephoned his mother again, from the Maxwell-Scott house, at about 12.15.

Later, said Mrs Maxwell-Scott, he asked for notepaper and wrote two letters. Mrs Maxwell-Scott watched him. Both letters were to Bill Shand Kydd. The first one read as follows:

Dear Bill,

The most ghastly circumstances arose tonight, which I have described briefly to my mother, when I interrupted the fight at Lower Belgrave Street and the man left.

V. accused me of having hired him. I took her upstairs and sent Frances to bed and tried to clean her up. She lay doggo for a bit. I went into the bathroom and she left the house.

The circumstantial evidence against me is strong in that V. will say it was all my doing and I will lie doggo for a while, but I am only concerned about the children. If you can manage it I would like them to live with you.

V. has demonstrated her hatred for me in the past and would do anything to see me accused.

For George and Frances to go through life knowing their father had been in the dock accused of attempted murder would be too much for them.

When they are old enough to understand explain to them the dream of paranoia and look after them.

Lucky

After that Mrs Maxwell-Scott tried to persuade Lucan to stay the night, and he almost gave in, but he then said that he must get back to clear things up. He did not mention London. Before he left he asked her to post the two letters and requested some sleeping pills, saying he was sure he would have difficulty in sleeping. She gave him four Valium, the best she could find. He left at about 1.15 a.m. She thought his car was a dark saloon. It was neither a Mini nor a sports car. After he had gone she went back to bed.

Mr Watling attacked Mrs Maxwell-Scott's evidence on rather curious lines. He wished to establish that she was a lawyer and that her evidence might therefore be misleading.

> *Mr Watling*: When Lord Lucan left that house, he knew or had been told that the nanny had been killed and his wife badly attacked. You are no doubt aware that no one has seen Lord Lucan since he left your house at 1.15 that morning?
>
> *A*: No one has said they have seen him. [*This guarded reply was enough to set Mr Watling off.*]
>
> *Q*: Is it right you are, in fact, a trained lawyer, a member of the Bar?
>
> *A*: I was called to the Bar nearly eighteen years ago but I never practised.
>
> *Q*: Your father was a lawyer? [*Worse and worse.*]
>
> *A*: My father was a lawyer.
>
> *Q*: Is it right that Lord Lucan at no time described to you that man he had seen attacking his wife?
>
> *A*: Not entirely right. Lord Lucan did not see him clearly enough to describe him. He said the man was large.

This was *not* the answer Mr Watling had been expecting. He had been trying to establish the flimsiness of Lucan's account. It was a minor example of asking one question too many, and Mr Watling sat down. Mrs Maxwell-Scott then passed into the gentler hands of Mr Eastham. She told Mr Eastham that Lucan was in a state of controlled shock. 'In my words, he obviously panicked and lost his head. He put it another way. He said he felt that there he was, alone in the house, the dead body, all that blood, a murderer that got away and a wife gone away who would almost certainly try to implicate him. He said no one would believe his story. He said the room was horrific with all the blood. I think he felt squeamish with all the blood.'

She had asked him whether anyone would be likely to want to kill Mrs Rivett and he had replied: 'No. It would not be anyone wanting to kill her. She was a very nice girl.' He had been speaking to the Official Solicitor about her and telling him how pleased he was with her. Mrs Maxwell-Scott concluded by saying, 'It was quite incredible that he should have had anything to do with it.'

The third witness who appeared and who was sympathetic to Lord Lucan was Bill Shand Kydd, company director, of Cambridge Street, London. He said that Lord Lucan was 'not one of my greatest friends, but I like him'. He had last seen him about two weeks before he disappeared. He had seemed relaxed and was looking forward to Christmas because it was his turn to have the children. Mr Shand Kydd said that Lord Lucan had been worried about the children and seemed to think that they were not being looked after. At this, counsel for Lady Lucan objected on the grounds that it was hearsay. The coroner upheld the objection. Mr Shand Kydd read out the two letters he had received from Lucan after the murder, which were postmarked Uckfield. Questioned by counsel for the police, he said that he had noticed the stains on the envelopes, realized they were blood and had pointed them out to the police.

Mr Eastham then asked him a series of questions concerning the letters which he should answer with either a 'yes' or a 'no', bearing in mind that Lady Lucan must not be discredited. Asked if he understood the phrase 'dream of paranoia', he said, 'Yes,' but he was not allowed to explain it. Mr Eastham also read out the phrase 'Veronica has demonstrated her hatred for me in the past' and asked Mr Shand Kydd if he could develop that and tell the jury more about it. 'Yes,' he replied. After giving his evidence Mr Shand Kydd was released from the rest of the hearing so that he could attend to 'important business'. The *Daily*

Mirror reported that he was seen on the following day in the Royal Enclosure at Ascot racecourse.

On the third day of the hearing the jury heard from another witness sympathetic to Lord Lucan. This was Michael Stoop. Not only had Stoop lent Lucan the car which was found abandoned in Newhaven, he had also received the last communication known to have been sent by him. Mr Stoop, described as a 53-year-old retired company director but better known as an expert backgammon player, said that he had known Lord Lucan for about fifteen years and that they were both members of the Clermont Club. More than two weeks before the murder, when he was at another gambling club, the Portland, Lucan had asked to borrow his Ford Corsair, which was a 'pretty dirty old banger'. Lord Lucan was to insure the car for himself. Mr Stoop arranged to leave the Ford, with the keys inside, for Lord Lucan to collect. He agreed that there was no lead piping in it at that time. On the Monday following the murder Mr Stoop called at a third club, the St James's Club, where he was handed an unstamped letter. The porter had had to pay the postage due. The letter read as follows:

My dear Michael,
  I have had a traumatic night of unbelievable coincidence. However I won't bore you with anything or involve you except to say that when you come across my children, which I hope you will, please tell them that you knew me and that all I cared about was them. The fact that a crooked solicitor and a rotten psychiatrist destroyed me between them will be of no importance to the children. I gave Bill Shand Kydd an account of what really happened, but judging by my last efforts in court no one, let alone a 67-year-old judge, would believe – and I no longer care, except that my children should be protected.
    Yours ever,
                        John

Mr Eastham asked Mr Stoop if, when he received the letter, he knew about the events at 46 Lower Belgrave Street and that Lucan was missing. Mr Stoop said, 'Yes.' He said that he had screwed up the envelope and thrown it into a wastepaper basket. He could not recall whether the envelope was handwritten, nor the postmark. There had been several letters and he had thrown away all the envelopes. Once he had read the letter he had contacted the police. Mr Eastham again used the device of 'yes' or 'no' answers. Mr Stoop said that the references to the solicitor, psychiatrist and judge were all associated with the custody case. Asked whether he understood the phrase 'I no longer care, except that my children should be protected', Mr Stoop replied that he could not deal with that by a 'yes' or 'no'. Mr Eastham then said, 'If I asked you against what or whom the children were to be protected, could you answer?', but the coroner, by now impatient, intervened to say that the question should be disregarded and the previous answer should be recorded.

Questioned by Mr Watling, Mr Stoop said that as far as he could remember the envelope had been 'a large, white, business-type envelope'. He then said that he thought he recognized the notepaper as being of the type he kept in the glove pocket of his car. He received the letter at about 4.45 p.m. and telephoned the police at Gerald Road at about 5 p.m. He asked the police if he should take the letter straight round and was told that it didn't matter and that he could take it the next time he was passing. Mr Watling queried this surprising suggestion. He asked whether it had not been Mr Stoop who said that he couldn't take it round because he had an important meeting to attend. Mr Stoop said he thought not. He agreed that he had eventually handed the letter in at 3 o'clock next morning. When the police discovered the envelope was missing they searched the dustbins of the St James's Club but found nothing, although there had been no refuse collection. It was the missing envelope of Michael Stoop's that finally persuaded Detective Chief Superintendent Ranson to apply for a warrant. The 'horseplay of the upper classes' was being taken too far. A few hours after Mr Ranson had read the letter, on Tuesday morning, a magistrate signed two warrants for Lucan's arrest, one for murder, the other for attempted murder.

Michael Stoop's evidence concluded the case, in so far as there was one, for Lord Lucan. Of the remaining witnesses out of the total of thirty-two, the most important were the police. Detective Chief Inspector David Gerring, second in command of the inquiry, said that on checking Lord Lucan's story the police had found 'no trace whatsoever' of the third person Lucan claimed to have disturbed. There were no signs of a fight in the front of the basement; there were no signs of forcible entry; and no one had been found with a key. Nor was there any trace of Lord Lucan, even though inquiries had been made 'in nearly every country in the world'.

Dr Margaret Pereira of the Metropolitan Police Laboratory, one of the world's leading experts on blood groups, said that she had found evidence of two violent attacks, one in the breakfast room in the basement, the other on the stairs leading from the hall. Blood stains in the basement were primarily of Group B, Sandra Rivett's group, shared by 8.5 per cent of the population; those on the ground floor were primarily of Group A, Lady Lucan's group, shared by 42 per cent of the population.* Blood had been splashed over walls, carpets and ceilings. Considerable force would have had to be used to cause the radiating pattern of blood found on the stairs; this may have been caused by a weapon striking a wound which

---

* So it was the nanny who was, in Tony Hancock's phrase, 'one of nature's aristocrats'.

was already bleeding. There was blood on the ceiling of an ante-room of the hall, probably spattered there by the weapon of an attacker. The piece of lead piping was 'grossly distorted', and the adhesive surgical tape around it was stained with blood from groups A and B. It was about 9 inches long and weighed 2¼ pounds. The victim on the stairs was battered by an attacker standing with his back to the ante-room.

In the Ford Corsair there was extensive blood smearing on both front seats, the interior of the passenger side front door, the dashboard, the map box and the steering wheel. Blood found on the driver's-side window was of Group B and that on the dashboard of Group A. Most of the blood stains were AB (a rare group found in 3 per cent of the population), or a mixture of two groups.

Questioned by Mr Eastham, Dr Pereira agreed that Lord Lucan would have had extensive blood stains on his clothes if he had run down to the basement, slipped in a pool of it and subsequently helped his wife up the stairs, as he had claimed. A smear of Group B blood beneath the arch of one of Lady Lucan's shoes could have been caused by her walking through the basement. The Group B blood stains on her clothes could have come from her attacker if he had been saturated with blood of that group or had himself been Group B. Questioned by Mr David Webster, for the Rivett family, Dr Pereira said that the evidence certainly suggested that the same piece of lead piping had been used to hit both women.

Questioned by Mr Watling, Dr Pereira said that she had found greyish-blue wool fibres, which were microscopically indistinguishable, on a bath towel, the wash-basin, the bludgeon, the basement and in the car. It was 'highly likely' that they had been left by the same person.

Dr Robert David, also of the Metropolitan Police Laboratory, said that in his opinion the piece of lead piping

found at No. 46 and the piece found in the car had been
cut from the same length. The piece found in the car was
also bandaged. It was 16½ inches long and weighed 4 lb
1 oz. Both pieces had traces, at one end, of light-blue and
royal-blue paint from a hacksaw blade. One piece was
more corroded, and there were indications that at one time
they had been water pipes. The differences in corrosion
could have been caused by different usage.

Mr Ian Lucas, a 'senior fingerprint officer' at New
Scotland Yard, said that prints found on the interior driving
mirror of the Ford and a print found in Lord Lucan's flat
had probably been made by the same person. Three marks
found in the car had not been eliminated, nine at Lord
Lucan's flat and twelve at No. 46. He could not say whose
prints they were. He had found no prints that could be
traced to Lord Lucan. All the prints found in the basement
at No. 46 had come from the Lucan children, Mrs Rivett or
police officers. Mr Watling established that this meant that
whoever had attacked Mrs Rivett had left no fingerprints.

The inquest also heard from Mr Genese, the moneylender in Bexleyheath, and from Mr Andrew Demetrio,
assistant restaurant manager at the Clermont Club, who
said that Lord Lucan had telephoned at about 8.30 p.m. to
reserve a table for four at 11 p.m. At 10.45 a party of four
people had turned up, including Mr Greville Howard and
his girlfriend, all of whom had been to the Mermaid
Theatre. They had said that Lord Lucan was coming to
join them and a fifth chair was brought to the table, but
Lord Lucan had never arrived. About fifteen minutes after
the telephone call, Lord Lucan had appeared at the Club.
He had spoken to the linkman, Billy Edgson, through the
lobby window, asked if his friends had arrived yet, and
then driven away in his Mercedes.

Earlier the foreman of the jury, Mr William Thomas,
said to the coroner: 'We have heard nothing at all from

Lady Lucan about the nanny being murdered. We heard about her going to the barman at the Plumber's Arms and saying to him, "He has murdered my nanny." How did she know the nanny had been murdered?' The coroner said they must wait until all the evidence had been heard, and he hoped to satisfy them then. In the event he was unable to do so. When the evidence was complete Dr Thurston sent the jury out while he discussed the question. He then told them that they must not speculate as to how it came about that this had been said. The difficulty was that in law Lady Lucan was barred from giving evidence against her husband except with regard to the attack on herself.

This was a prime example of the disadvantage of having two tribunals, acting under different rules of evidence, dealing with the same crime. What the jury was prevented from knowing was that in her statement to the police, which was made over a period of two days, Lady Lucan had said that after he had stopped attacking her, Lord Lucan had told her that he had murdered the nanny. He then told her that the killing had been a mistake and that he had intended to murder her.

Mr Eastham, for Lord Lucan's mother, had objected that if this evidence were allowed, it would be 'absolutely devastating'. If Lord Lucan were to reappear, 'It would debar him from a fair trial.' Even Mr Watling, for the police, took no more than a 'neutral line' on the question. But he pointed out that Mr Eastham had laid great emphasis on Lord Lucan's version, the presence of a third person, and that the jury must not be left with the impression that Lady Lucan had found out about the nanny's murder as a result of being in a fight in the basement and seeing the sack with the body in it. In response to Mr Watling's argument the coroner eventually told the jury that it must consider very carefully the possibility of a third party, which was Lord Lucan's version of events, and that the evidence for it was mainly hearsay.

The coroner also ruled out other important evidence, the statement by Greville Howard. Again there was legal argument, which Mr Eastham won. Mr Howard had reported the conversation that he had had with Lord Lucan some months earlier, when Lucan had spoken of getting rid of Veronica and dumping her body in the Solent. Mr Eastham objected to this statement being read in court because Mr Howard was in hospital, and although he had been called as a witness, he was unable to be present and could not therefore be questioned on the statement. This time Mr Watling did not take a neutral line. He said that it was 'highly relevant evidence, which ought to be laid before the jury'. Mr Eastham continued to insist that it was prejudicial, and in the event the coroner was persuaded to exclude the statement.

On the fourth day of the inquest Dr Thurston began his summing up. As on every previous day, Lady Lucan sat immediately behind her mother-in-law, alone except for her police bodyguard. The fact that the two women, bearing the same title, had sat like this throughout the proceedings, exchanging neither word nor glance, had become obvious to everyone, and the coroner drew the jury's attention to the hostile atmosphere in which the case had been conducted.

'You know Lord and Lady Lucan are separated,' he said. 'They have been on either side of custody proceedings. It is fairly clear from Lord Lucan's letters that there is existing in the family animosity, tension and matters which, if heard, could only be prejudicial. They could cause pain to the persons concerned if aired. The airing of family tensions would not benefit this inquiry, and to turn this into a family forum to air those tensions would be a wrong thing.'

The scientific evidence, said Dr Thurston, supported the statement made by Lady Lucan. As regards Lord Lucan's version, in so far as that could be given, the coroner pointed out that he had not tried to telephone the police and ambulance immediately and wondered whether, if he had simply been trying to help, his wife would have run to the pub crying 'Murder!' The coroner's summing-up lasted seventy minutes, after which the jury retired. Mr Albert Hensby, Mrs Rivett's father, who had sat silently at the back of the court for four days, wondering why his daughter's name was hardly mentioned, was not in court when the jury returned after only thirty-one minutes. So he did not hear the foreman say that their verdict was that the cause of Sandra Rivett's death was 'murder, by Lord Lucan'.

After the hearing Lady Lucan said that she was neither pleased nor displeased with the verdict. 'I was only concerned with establishing the facts,' she said.

Mr Hensby was reported in the *Guardian* as wishing to forget about the whole business and especially about the closed circle of people around Lord Lucan which his family had come up against.

The Rev. William Gibbs, who was married to Lady Sarah Gibbs, Lucan's sister, said, 'To me it is frightening that a coroner's court can name a man a murderer without hearing all the relevant evidence. The family will investigate what legal steps can be taken to clear Lord Lucan's name. My wife and I are firmly convinced that he is not guilty of murder. We will do anything in our power to prove this.'

And Detective Chief Superintendent Roy Ranson said, 'The verdict makes no difference. He would have been charged whatever the verdict. My personal feelings are that he's dead. The search will go on until we find him — dead or alive.' The police revealed that in addition to the thirty-two witnesses who had appeared at the inquest there were an additional sixty-one witnesses in the case. Chief Superintendent Ranson left the inquiry and switched his attention to a London homosexual murder, where his efforts, whatever the outcome, were never likely to attract so much attention.

The Dowager Countess of Lucan returned to the obscurity of her undeniably useful life. Her death in 1985 was marked by a brief obituary in *The Times*, which referred to her husband and to her own time as a local Labour councillor. But her chief claim to readers' attention was as 'mother of the 7th Earl of Lucan, who disappeared in 1974 after the murder of his family's nanny, Miss Sandra Rivett'. Not even then could they get Mrs Rivett's name right.

The inquest into the death of Sandra Rivett was an historic occasion and a legal oddity. It was the last time a coroner's jury was invited to name a murderer; the right was abolished by the Criminal Law Act of 1977 as a direct result of this case. The procedure adopted by the coroner, Dr Gavin Thurston, had been that in settling the question of who had killed Sandra Rivett no evidence in discredit of the witnesses present would be allowed. Since the prosecution witnesses were mostly present and could not be attacked, whereas witnesses for the defence were mostly absent, this ruling had the consequence that only the prosecution side of the case could be heard. The police and forensic experts mainly gave evidence as to the state of the house and the car; their credit was unchallenged. The only eyewitness fatal to Lord Lucan was his wife, and her credit could not be challenged. But it was an essential part of Lucan's defence that Veronica Lucan's evidence should be challenged. Since this could not be done, the proceedings, regarded as a trial, were hopelessly unfair. It was an example of the adversary system of trial in which one of the protagonists had to fight unarmed. If the circumstances were to arise again today, the coroner's jury could still bring in a verdict of murder, but it would not be allowed to name a murderer. The identity of the presumed killer would be known only if there was a police warrant out for his arrest.

Contested as it was, under the old rules, the Sandra Rivett inquest was the equivalent of summary proceedings in a magistrate's court. But whereas such proceedings result in a committal for trial, an inquest results in the verdict of a jury. There lay the unfairness. It is normal for the prosecution's case to go largely unanswered in proceedings that lead to a committal; a committal bears no implication of guilt for the accused. He still awaits his trial. But the verdict of a jury, even a coroner's jury, is a judgement. In the public mind Lucan was found guilty of murder at the inquest, even though he was absent, undefended and untried. Strangely enough, this glaring injustice aroused no public comment or anxiety at the time. 'I have prayed for three days and three nights for this verdict,' said Mrs Eunice Hensby, after the case. 'I have lived in fear that they would say my daughter was murdered by someone unknown.' She would have considered *that* the injustice, and a victory for privilege, and by and large the public agreed with her. As a result of the verdict at the inquest, Lucan now stands committed for trial for murder at the Old Bailey on evidence provided more than twelve years ago. The lucidity or fallibility of the witnesses today is less of an issue than it would have been if summary proceedings had still to take place. He has, in effect, been tried and convicted in his absence.

CHAPTER SIX

Beyond the Pale

Where be your gibes now? Your gambols? Your songs?
Your flashes of merriment, that were wont to set the
table on a roar?

Shakespeare, *Hamlet*, Act V, Sc. 1

Two events were decisive for that group of people known
as the 'Clermont set', but who might have been better
termed 'Lucan's friends', in June 1975. The first was the
article by James Fox in the *Sunday Times Magazine*, which
set the scene for the inquest, was strongly sympathetic to
Lady Lucan and treated the wealthy gambling friends of
Lucan with some contempt. The second event was the
inquest itself. For the friends of John Lucan the inquest
was a rearguard action, which ended in defeat. The verdict
could not have been worse, and they were presented to the
public as heartless, selfish and idle, people who put their
friend's family name above normal human decency.
Aspinall's phrase for individual members of the common
people, 'elements of the urban biomass', was taken up and
turned against them.

Many of Lord Lucan's friends were quite as appalled by

the murder of Sandra Rivett as any card-carrying humanitarian, and Lucan's family could hardly be blamed for attempting to represent his interests in his absence. But they were hampered in their efforts by their own uncertainty and by the peculiar rules of evidence which allowed a prosecution case to be presented in public, and a verdict to be reached, in the absence of any adequate case for the defence.

A tragedy now took place within the magic circle. Hating the exposed position in which they found themselves, stung by the contemptuous terms in which they were described and outraged by what they considered to be a travesty of justice with regard to the proper outcome of the dispute between John and Veronica Lucan, some of John Lucan's friends looked around for a scapegoat. A suitable victim was not hard to find. The *Sunday Times* article had appeared on 6 June. On 17 June, the morning the inquest opened, Dominick Elwes received a letter from Annabel Birley's son, Robin – then still a schoolboy at Eton – accusing him of selling private photographs of his mother to the *Sunday Times*. Elwes and the writer of the article, James Fox, both denied this, but persecution of Elwes followed. By the end of the week Mark Birley had barred Elwes from Annabel's, in the basement of the Clermont Club, and from another of his houses, and had issued writs against him for two trifling debts. It was a schoolboy level of cruelty that proved highly effective. Elwes was reduced to tears and Daniel Meinertzhagen, considering that Elwes was on the verge of a nervous breakdown, sent him to stay with friends in the South of France and Spain. In August Elwes returned to England to find his former friends implacable. Elwes had suffered from manic depression for years and had attempted suicide before. He killed himself in September.

Early the following December a letter arrived at 114

Mount Street, the Mayfair headquarters, in England, of the Society of Jesus. It was addressed to the Provincial of the Jesuits.

> Dear Rev. Father,
>   I would refer you to the recently held memorial service for the late Mr Dominick Elwes at your church.
>   This did seem to attract a fair number of the 'high-class scum' that are continually publicized in the gutter press, and among whom Mr Elwes seemed to have fallen. It was good to see them on their knees, in fact if not in spirit, though one wished that our society could be cleansed of such vermin or that they could be put to a useful service for humanity.
>   As a Socialist I pontificate, however, so to the point of this screed. I was astounded to hear somebody by the name of John Aspinall, with private money of course – a former gambler and now a keeper of wild animals – 'ham' his way through a most tasteless oration for which a Mr Tremayne Rodd quite rightly thumped him.
>   As a practising Roman Catholic for the last 50 years, I never realised that this was allowed, and therefore wondered whether this is common practice with you or whether an exception had been made in this 'gentleman's' case.
>   I must admit to great expectations of the memorial service for the late (?) Lord Lucan, should it ever be held in your church. The attendance will no doubt be the same, together with other specimens of this class, who at least give some justification for a strong Communist party!
>   Yours sincerely,
>   A. G. Hughes

This letter was answered in due course by Father O'Callaghan, S J, who decided to take it at face value. 'On the occasion referred to,' Father O'Callaghan explained, 'the Elwes family asked if a layman might give the address without telling anyone here who it was, so that we were presented with the *fait accompli* on the morning itself. Maybe an error of judgement was made by my not asking. If so I take the full responsibility.' Father O'Callaghan finished with a flourish. 'However, not having any political axe to grind, I seem to recall that Our Lord was often blamed for associating with those considered at that time to be "sinners" ... harlots, tax-collectors, and thieves. Being a member of His Company, one tries, in little ways, to be like him.'

The point at which the feelings of these correspondents met was in the wish to distance themselves from the members of the congregation who attended the memorial service for Dominick Elwes, a desire which was as clearly expressed in Father O'Callaghan's rather unconvincing picture of Farm Street as a devout, aristocratic thieves' kitchen as it was in the vituperation of A. G. Hughes. But in the exchange of letters between the 'pontificating Socialist' and the bemused and placating Jesuit one can see the emergence of another pattern: the transformation of a tragedy into farce, an unintended consequence of the desperate act of self-slaughter, itself the hideous and unimagined sequel to the determination of a determined father to regain custody of his young children.

In fact, most of the service had been routine. True, it was conducted by Fr Peter Blake – 'Hell-Fire Blake' – a curious choice, since he was the priest who had usually been selected by the Benedictines of Downside Abbey to preach the annual Lent retreat to little Dominick. True, it had been preceded by lines printed in *The Times*, headed 'A Farewell for Dominick by C. E.', which ended:

... For the wild winds of Autumn have flown
You fleet upon their storm-horses, beyond the galaxies of
     Time,
Yet it is you who truly live – and us, the forgotten
     dream ...

But the only really odd aspect had been the bluntness of the two lay addresses. In the first, given by Ken Tynan, Elwes was described as a 'romantic monarchist'. 'He loved the world of wealth and ceremony far more than it deserved,' said Tynan. Certain people had elected him their court jester and he happily embraced this role. But they never really accepted him because, in the final analysis, he did not have quite enough money. 'It may be that he set too much store by the favourable opinions of people, many of whom were manifestly his inferiors. Towards the end of his life he said to me with a grin of self-deprecation: "I thought I was a hermit and I found I was a pariah." '

The second address was given by one of that very group which had elected Elwes as its jester, a friend of Elwes, though not of Tynan. Aspinall at that moment was rather in the position of Hamlet or Prince Hal reminiscing about Yorick or Falstaff, but he behaved more like Hal than Hamlet. He said of Elwes: 'He resented the fact that many lesser men had found fame through the media and through the newspapers. He knew many people who had achieved much, but he never managed it. His business affairs had never been the success they might have been. He was happiest entertaining a dozen or more close friends with his amusing stories or his wit. But, unfortunately, modern society does not repay someone like him. It is the man who can entertain television audiences with his banalities who gets its rewards.'

Coming as it did at a requiem mass for a man who had committed suicide through despair over his debts and the ostracism of his friends and the withdrawal of their patronage and credit, people of whom Aspinall was an intimate, all of this seemed insufferably smug and heartless to many members of the congregation. One of Elwes's cousins, Tremayne Rodd, acted for many when he

punched Aspinall on the jaw after the ceremony and said,
'That's what I think of your bloody speech, Aspinall.' It
was a blow that was to lead to almost as many unintended
consequences as any of those struck one year earlier in
Lower Belgrave Street. 'Right hook ends the memorial
service to man from Lucan Set' was how the *Daily Mail*
told it. No doubt this was an accurate summary of public
interest, although in his least optimistic moments B. E. D.
Elwes might have been surprised to know that in the
headlines over a report of his memorial service he was
remembered as 'man from Lucan Set'. He would, however,
have been delighted that his memorial service had made
the headlines.

The cause of all this bother, Dominick Elwes, had been
a brilliant man, a creature of the 1950s to the end. But the
end had been preceded by persecution. Two months before
he died the *Daily Express* printed as its lead story a pathetic
interview with him from St-Jean-Cap-Ferrat. 'If Lucky is
still alive, as I believe he is, would he please contact me,'
Elwes was reported as saying. The interview took place in
the right setting, the Villa Paladium, owned by Earl Compton, but the *Express* reporters said that Elwes was too
nervous to sip his drink. He just fidgeted with the glass.
Inventing a purpose for this article, the *Express* said:
'French police along the Riviera's golden coastline have
been warned to expect Lord Lucan to make a dash for it
aboard a yacht from here, if he is in France. "I suppose I
am one of his best friends," said Mr Elwes, 42. "Every day
during our fifteen years of friendship we have always been
in daily touch – we were almost like brothers . . . I am sure
he is still alive somewhere and hiding in the most desperate
circumstances . . . Why, oh why, doesn't he get in touch
with any of us? We all have our personal problems but we
still feel Lucky needs help badly . . . We are all prepared to
accept his alibi and help him in every way possible . . . I've

been so worried about Lucky that I've almost reached a state of depression. He must telephone me. Why doesn't he get in touch with me? My other friends in London realize the sort of pressure I've been under. This is a ghastly business with police asking me questions all the time. My good friend Lord Compton offered me this refuge to disappear to. I still cannot relax even though I am totally alone. I feel so lost." ' In this story Elwes was described as 'Chelsea artist'. The other oddity was that Lucan had never publicly offered the alibi Elwes spoke of. So far from being 'elsewhere', Lucan had put forward an explanation for being on the spot.

Though the *Daily Express* story gave a vivid impression of Elwes's misery, it did not explain the reasons for it. But something in Elwes's account of his interviews with the police had a familiar ring to it of far-off schooldays, of being in continual trouble with the headmaster ('asking me questions all the time'). The police had indeed found Elwes by far the most sensitive and impressionable of Lucan's close friends. They took the view that if anyone in the group would talk, it would be Elwes, and they gave him a hard time.

Elwes was always, according to some, 'suicide material', having been unstable and unsuccessful and far too 'up-and-down' for his own good. He had wonderful talent as a mimic and entertainer, and he sold his paintings, but he was mainly just the funniest person in the room, and that is both a demanding and a badly paid occupation. 'He could never find the fame to which he knew he was entitled,' said Aspinall from the pulpit in Farm Street. But is anyone 'entitled' to fame? Certainly the pulpit of a Catholic church during a memorial service seems an odd place to put forward the idea. And what sort of fame? Presumably Elwes did not want Lucan's fame, for instance. And was he indeed obsessed with 'fame', as opposed to the recognition, for instance, of his friends, social success, the wealth which could have made him an independent agent? Does one see Dominick Elwes sitting in the gloom of his little flat saying, 'If only I had the fame which is my due. I am wasting my substance. I am casting my pearls before swine.' Perhaps one does.

But after the murder there was at least the Press. For once Elwes really was in the thick of it. He had attended Aspinall's lunch; he had been sent round to St George's Hospital. Elwes had known the Press for a long time – the publicity for his own elopement had been masterminded by an *Express* reporter – and he was confident that he could turn the general interest to his advantage. When James Fox asked to speak to him, on behalf of the *Sunday Times*, Elwes did not hesitate and he proved helpful to Fox, though not exceptionally so; Aspinall, for instance, talked to Fox at even greater length. But then came the offer that was to lead to Elwes's suicide: £200 to paint for the *Sunday Times* a picture of the 'Clermont set' in the Clermont.

Elwes did a large group portrait. It verged on caricature, but it would not have caused offence except for certain other aspects of the article which were outside his control. One was the line Fox took – very pro-Veronica and derisive of the 'Clermont set'. They simply hadn't realized quite what an unsympathetic appearance they gave to the rest of the world. And there was Elwes's contributing a portrait, so placing himself on the other side of the green-baize door, the jester as social critic. The final fatal ingredient was the photographs Fox obtained to illustrate his piece. They were private family snaps, and no one would admit to supplying them. But Elwes's portrait, as part of the same series, made him the jester as Judas.

The most 'embarrassing' photographs in the series, the only ones that could not have come from Veronica Lucan's album, were taken on a holiday in Acapulco in March 1973. Present were Goldsmith and Annabel Birley, Peter West, Elwes and Lucan. (They were taken a few weeks after Lucan had left his wife.) The cover showed Lucan with Annabel Birley, who was dressed in a bikini, in light-hearted pose. Without pausing to make any further inquiries (the most obvious and perfectly proper source of the photos was, after all, the police), Mark Birley, Annabel Birley and Jimmy Goldsmith decided that Elwes had betrayed their hospitality. He was beyond the pale, in his own words 'a pariah'; he was to be blackballed in the fine old tradition of clubland and the gaming houses. He was banned from the Clermont, Annabel's and Mark's Restaurant. Writs went out. For Elwes, a manic-depressive, sick, with heavy debts, his father dying, himself under police pressure and suffering from a loss of self-confidence, it was the end of the line. One of his suicide notes read, 'I hope A, M and J are happy now.'

As a result of John Lucan's decision to leap into action and recover his children, a second onlooker had died, this time one of his best friends.

PART TWO

The Man who Wanted to Own a Newspaper

Everybody in the world thinks we're going down the tubes. And we're doing so well, I'm laughing my ass off. We're making so much money I can't count it.

> Florida bullion dealer under investigation
> by the *Wall Street Journal*, 1983

CHAPTER SEVEN

Mr Ranson's Previous Case

If Lord Lucan had ever been tried for murder, it would have been at the Old Bailey, almost certainly in No. 1 Court, usually the scene of the more notorious trials. It was in the dock of No. 1 Court that the murderer Dr Crippen and the traitor William Joyce, among many others, were last seen in public before being 'taken down' to execution. So it was with some surprise, on a fine morning in May 1977, that I found myself standing in this same dock, wondering how I had got there at last.

It had not been easily achieved. It was, indeed, one of the many unintended consequences of Lucan's decision to spring into action. The deeds which should have led to Lucan's peering over the rail on to the wigs of the lawyers some distance below had eventually caused me and Richard Ingrams, the editor of *Private Eye*, to be standing there instead. The murder of Mrs Rivett, the report in the *Sunday Times Magazine*, the verdict of the coroner's jury, the persecution and suicide of Dominick Elwes, John Aspinall's address at Elwes's memorial service and Tremayne Rodd's momentary loss of composure had all led to an article which I had written for *Private Eye* in December 1975. And it was that article which led eventually to No. 1 Court, the Old Bailey.

Private Eye in 1975 was still at the height of its reputation as a journal of disclosure, still basking in the glory of 'Footnotes', the disturbingly well-informed news column written by Paul Foot. The fortnightly paper was seen as a 'dangerous' newspaper in the tradition of John Wilkes, a paper that was prepared to take risks in dealing with serious issues and was beyond the reach of those who normally govern the press. Threats of libel actions were of little use against *Private Eye*; the more cases the paper lost, the more it seemed to flourish. When it had been invited to join the 'D' Notice scheme in 1964 it had accepted enthusiastically, offering to print any official secrets that it received. It derived only a small proportion of its income from advertising. Its staff belonged to no government lobby. Its opinions were a rich and ill-assorted mixture of politics, faiths and scepticisms. *Private Eye* seemed to be beyond control.

At the time when the article about the death of Dominick Elwes appeared *Private Eye* was chiefly distracted by a very different topic, the question of whether the Prime Minister, Harold Wilson, was or was not a KGB agent. The two stories, apparently containing nothing in common, were eventually to combine against the *Eye* in an unexpected way. When they did so it was the first time that the paper had, effectively, been silenced.

It had been in 1974 that Harold Wilson had announced that he had asked the police to investigate the theft, from his house in Lord North Street, of several bundles of tax records. It was apparently Mr Wilson's conviction that these papers had been stolen by a 'dirty tricks department' intent on creating a British Watergate scandal by which they hoped to discredit both Wilson and other members of the Labour Cabinet.

It was not clear why the Prime Minister should suggest that publication of his income-tax papers could cause a political scandal, but 1974 was an unusual year. The Arab–Israeli War of October 1973 had led to the international oil crisis. In Britain the National Union of Mineworkers had seized the opportunity to strike and had then provoked a succession of national crises, leading to the three-day week and the fall of the Conservative government. There had been two general elections, fought largely on the issue of trade-union power, and the trade union movement had won. It was true that Harold Wilson's majority was only three, but he declared this to be 'workable' and set to work.

For the right the lesson was clear. The fat days of the property boom were over for good. The trade unions were able to write their own terms. The country was in the hands of the communists. One result was a growing number of rumours concerning those in high places. Two general elections had settled nothing; they had served only to make matters much worse. The rumours were further encouraged when the Prime Minister complained not only that his home had been burgled but also that his office at 10 Downing Street was bugged by MI5. As a matter of fact, although he lacked the necessary proof at the time, the Prime Minister was right; he *was* being investigated by the Security Service. He did not have the evidence to prove this, but *Private Eye* magazine had already begun to acquire it.

During the years of Opposition between 1970 and 1974 Wilson had opened a 'private office' which had been funded in secret by a group of wealthy political supporters and lobbyists. At that time the amount available from public money was inadequate to meet the expenses of the leader of the Opposition; the purpose of Wilson's 'secret fund' was to bridge the gap. The first chairman of the fund was Wilfred Brown (Lord Brown, 1964), an industrialist and former junior minister. Then there was Arnold Goodman (Lord Goodman, 1964), who had once been Wilson's solicitor, and Sir Samuel Fisher (Lord Fisher, 1974), who had been a friend of Wilson for years and was a former Labour local councillor. There was nothing surprising about these names. But questions were raised because of the secrecy surrounding the fund – not even the Labour Party knew of its leader's chosen method of paying for his office. Lord Brown explained this by saying that if the Labour Party had known about it, they 'would have wanted to get their fingers into it'.

Secondly, the full list of contributors, said to number about twelve, was never published. Wilson could never see that this was bound to arouse suspicions. It was eventually discovered that one of his benefactors was Rudy Sternberg (Sir Rudy 1970; Lord Plurenden, 1975); another trustee was Arieh L. Handler, the manager of the London branch of a Swiss bank. Needless to say, it was a Swiss bank, the International Credit Bank of Geneva, that later ran into trouble. Its London accounts were frozen in November 1974, and it was only then that news of the fund began to leak out. Some of the fund's money was paid through this bank. Lord Plurenden said, through his solicitor, that he had contributed £2,000 a year for four years, and that he had been recruited to the trust by Beattie Plummer, the widow of Sir Leslie Plummer, MP. Lady Plummer's name was one of those mentioned more than once in the MI5 documents which were at this time being leaked to *Private Eye*.

The arrangement of the private fund was characteristic of Harold Wilson. It was shrouded in a secrecy that was either quite unnecessary or deeply sinister. It was also needlessly complicated. When Mr Callaghan succeeded Wilson as leader of the Labour Party he discharged his expenses by soliciting contributions from the TUC and the Co-Operative Party. Any money donated privately was paid into Labour Party accounts against an official receipt from the Treasurer. Mr Callaghan did not apparently mind the Labour Party 'getting their fingers into it'. But as a result of Wilson's obsessive secrecy, and given the information in the MI5 documents, the idea got about that Harold Wilson enjoyed the company of a number of people who were either dubious customers or agents of a foreign power or both. The eventual casualty list among this group was to provide some substance for these critical suggestions.

As though that were not enough, rumours concerning the leader of the Liberal Party, Jeremy Thorpe, also began to spread, and the possibility that a charge of conspiracy to murder might be laid against one of the country's three leading party politicians was suggested. Finally, there was the disappearance, in mysterious circumstances, of John Stonehouse, a former Labour minister who had faked his own death, leaving a complicated financial mess behind him. Seen from the Clermont Club, the country was starting to resemble the less stable years of the Weimar Republic. Sir James Goldsmith began to develop his theory of 'the Communist infiltration of the Western media' and found a sympathetic audience in Berkeley Square. Nor was it just national political developments that were causing alarm. There was also the Portuguese revolution. Over the smoked salmon and lamb cutlets the talk turned, topically enough, to the pros and cons of a British military coup.

There had been two recent occasions when a military coup had been discussed in public. Jeremy Thorpe, at the time of the Rhodesian rebellion in 1966, had spoken of the need for 'pin-point' bombing. Wilson had rejected the idea of a military expedition, but in reaction to Thorpe's suggestion there was much talk of 'kith and kin', and doubts were raised about the loyalty of the armed forces if ordered to attack white Rhodesians.

From then it was not long before the left saw the armoured personnel carriers rolling down Whitehall. Meanwhile, out in Salisbury, General Sir Walter Walker formed his Concerned Citizens Vigilante Association, which was dedicated to exterminating communism in Wiltshire, and Colonel David Stirling called for public-spirited volunteers to join his private army, a force which would imitate the volunteers who had manned essential services during the General Strike, and who would cross picket lines to keep the country on the move. Michael Stoop was among those who joined.

Others worked on the possibility of a political coup. They included right-wing Tory politicians such as Airey Neave, a former MI5 officer, and a group of serving MI5 officers who, according to Peter Wright, one of their colleagues, decided to act on their common belief that the Labour Party had been infiltrated at the highest levels by the KGB. They were supported by 'a right-wing financier'. In May 1987 a Labour MP tabled a House of Commons motion in which he named this financier as Sir James Goldsmith. Goldsmith promptly denied it. He said that he had never met Peter Wright and that it was 'complete lunacy' to suggest that he had discussed the use of MI5 information with MI5 officers. Nineteen seventy-four was a time when many of the shrewdest and hardest-headed people in the country, as well as Lord Lucan, became obsessed with private illusion. But other extraordinary suggestions were based on fact. There was, for instance, the succession of casualties among the Prime Minister's chosen sponsors.

For *Private Eye* the story had started some years earlier

with a telephone call from one of Wilson's private staff. He was followed by a second Wilson aide and then by a third. All three had more or less the same story to tell, and one of them suggested that we should approach George Wigg, who had been a minister with special responsibility for security in the first Wilson administration of 1964.

At the time of his political power Colonel Wigg had been a particular target for *Private Eye*, and the idea of his co-operation seemed unlikely, but, strangely enough, when he was approached he seemed happy, even eager, to help. Unknown to us at the time, Wigg too was a former member of MI5. By 1974 he was a rather diminished figure living in a basement in Pimlico. He had become Lord Wigg, but he had lost all influence over Wilson. He made it quite clear, in our conversation, that he had been nobbled by Marcia Williams, Wilson's powerful private secretary. I asked him whether he lived alone, and he said that he went home to Stoke-on-Trent at weekends. His wife lived there all the time but she had always hated London and the political life; she was much happier in Stoke. Wigg was rather pathetic down in his basement, coming up for air to the pavement, where he would patrol slowly and aimlessly backwards and forwards glaring at passers-by, a familiar sight in the neighbourhood. He seemed out of things, but he retained one burning political ambition and that was to encompass the downfall of his old enemy Marcia Williams. The subject of our talk was the passages in his autobiography which she had managed to have removed. He and his publishers had been forced to agree to this, so he had decided to get them published, far more prominently, in *Private Eye*, as follows.

Here are two of the passages which Mrs Williams was so anxious to suppress. The first (from page 312) is Lord Wigg's estimate of her influence over Wilson, based on his two years' experience as Paymaster General in 10 Downing Street.

> His [Wilson's] dream world, as I saw it develop, was encouraged by his Personal Secretary, Mrs Marcia Williams. Like every energetic secretary whose methods of working are not under strict control she had become accustomed to taking day-to-day decisions for her boss. Now she indulged, in No. 10 Downing Street, the personal belief that she was a political genius and the power behind the throne. Looking back, those first few months in No. 10 possess a nightmarish quality. The Prime Minister, beset with public cares and great political problems, had too much of his time taken up by Mrs Williams and her problems, including her reactions to Government policy.

The significant cut in the second passage was on pp. 315–16.

> Unfortunately, Mrs Williams' growing influence was not, in my view, exercised with wisdom or restraint. It disturbed the very competent Private Office in No. 10 and led to unhappiness among men and women of great ability and complete loyalty. On the Prime Minister's own staff, many of them transferred from and paid for by Transport House, were a number who were also made unhappy. It became part of my job to dry the tears of many devoted people who could not keep up with *la politique de la maison*. Mrs Williams, no doubt through kindness of heart, also brought individuals on to the staff of No. 10 who, with complete fairness, could be described only as misfits. There is no doubt that the Prime Minister regarded Mrs Williams' opinion as being important; whatever the question under review, her reactions brought marked influence to bear on his thinking. It was the methodology of a man never strong in his power to take and implement decisions who was beginning to weaken under the pressures around him – and the influence exercised by Mrs Williams inside No.

10 was great and pervasive. It extended over the whole range of Government posts, including, of course, the selection of Ministers. As Mrs Williams said in 1967: 'Who does George Wigg think he is? I've forgotten more secrets than he'll ever know.' I was, however, a Member of the Government and a Member of the Privy Council; I saw Cabinet papers and a wide range of sensitive documents. The inference was that Mrs Williams saw and heard everything.

I did not dispute her statement then. I do not dispute it now.

'Don't worry, chum,' said Wigg as our conversation ended, 'I'm just sitting here in my hide-out, squinting down my sights. One day . . . *ping!*' Sadly enough for Lord Wigg, holed up in his Pimlico basement, things did not quite work out the way he dreamed. Some years later he regained the attention of the public when he was charged with kerb-crawling, soliciting women from his motor car. This was a rather draconian punishment for an elderly and harmless old soldier, formerly a man of some public distinction, even if it were true. But the possibility remained that he had been in some way set up. Not *ping! Bing!*

After our talk Lord Wigg drove me in his Rover saloon to Park Lane, where he may have been intending to amuse himself in a casino – he was chairman of the Horserace Betting Levy Board at the time – and before we parted he raised the subject of Lord Brayley, then Minister for the Army. He said that he had borrowed some money from Brayley. Perhaps he thought this was something *Private Eye* might already know about, and he did not want it to be thought that he was trying to conceal the debt. If so, he flattered us.

Of all Wilson's peculiar appointments, whether official or private, Colonel Lord Brayley was one of the strangest. He was the chairman of a small glass-bottle manufacturing company, not a particularly wealthy man. He was not close to Wilson but he had become a friend of Marcia. His qualification to be the political director of the Army seemed to be that he had served in it, without any particular distinction, during the last war. He had been given his peerage by Wilson expressly so that he could become Under-Secretary at the Ministry of Defence. Shortly after Brayley's appointment, *Private Eye* received the following illiterate but vivid letter from someone who apparently knew him but was not an admirer:

Dear Sir,
The arrogant, bad-tempered, Big-I-Am, bullish, conceited, cunning, demanding, egotistical, heavy-drinking, ill-mannered, insolent, self-opinioned and self-seeking Lord Brayley is yet another Minister who is not short on accommodation. He has two luxuriously furnished flats in exclusive Arlington House, a magnificent house near Oxford, well guarded and furnished with antiques, and a home in Cornwall . . .

What puzzles people who know him (but no one really gets to know Brayley, not even Harold Wilson) is that pre-war Desmond went into the Army with empty pockets and then after the war ended the Colonel suddenly became known as a wealthy man and in a very short time as a millionaire and art collector. Incidentally, he was one of those types who used his Army rank and he had a way of making people address him as Colonel and he became deaf if you called him Mister Brayley. People wondered how he suddenly acquired a collection of objets d'art. He acquired a reputation of being lavish with money, as though it had gone out of fashion.

PRIVATE EYE mentioned Brayley's jade collection but 'EYE' probably did not appreciate that the former Colonel's jade collection is worth more than £2 million

The front door of No. 46 Lower Belgrave Street.

(*Right*) 5 Eaton Row, the mews house behind No. 46.

(*Below*) Grants Hill House, Uckfield, Sussex, home of Mrs Susan Maxwell-Scott, the last person to see Lord Lucan.

(*Above*) Murder Squad detectives searching boats in Newhaven, 11 November 1974.

(*Below*) Detective Chief Superintendent Roy Ranson, in charge of the 'Lucan murder' inquiry, seen here in June 1975.

(*Above*) Sandra Rivett's father leaves after the inquest with Mrs Vera Ward, Sandra's aunt.

(*Opposite*) Lady Lucan after the jury at the inquest had named Lord Lucan as the murderer of Sandra Rivett.

Lord Lucan's mother, the Dowager Countess of Lucan, and his friend Bill Shand Kydd, who both gave evidence at the inquest into the death of Sandra Rivett.

Ian and Susan Maxwell-Scott arriving at the Westminster inquest.

Tessa Kennedy and Dominick Elwes in Havana, Cuba, after their elopement, 5 February 1958.

James Goldsmith and Isabel Patino after their marriage in 1953.

(*Above*) Charles Benson (*centre*) and
Stephen Raphael (*right*) playing
backgammon.

(*Right*) John Aspinall, outside the
Jesuit church in Farm Street. He has
just been punched following Dominick
Elwes's memorial service in 1975.

and, according to him, it is one of the finest in the world. Although he is usually tight-lipped about his possessions the other Brayley, the inebriated Desmond, talks about his collection.

Perhaps the closest person to Brayley is his chauffeur-valet, My Lord's former batman. He seems to have a special affinity to a motley group of war-time daredevils who served under his command – perhaps they re-live their exploits around the fireplace, recalling the daring tricks they got up to. The new Minister of the Army has always led a covert life but on occasions he likes to surround himself with VIPs at parties in his Arlington House flat or at his home near Oxford. You have to be real special to merit an invitation and you have to be extra special to be invited on the Brayley yacht.

He is never seen in the company of women, preferring to be with men, the famous, but he is really at home with his wartime buddies. He treats ordinary people, such as waiters and clerks, as inferiors. Ol' steel eyes Brayley can really send the shivers down your spine and when he's in an angry mood he barks, snarls and growls. Beware of the wrath of Brayley! Where does he eat? At the Caprice, Ritz, Dorchester, Savoy, Connaught, at the House of Lords and perhaps with Harold Wilson. He's a great friend of Marcia (and what a team they would make). By the way, how many times has Lord Brayley spoken in the House of Lords since he has taken his seat and since becoming Minister for the Army?

Unfortunately, the letter was unsigned. My suspicion at the time was that this highly coloured portrait may have been painted by the Colonel in person, in a last desperate bid to raise some cash via the libel courts, but if he had been hoping that *Private Eye* would publish the letter as it stood, he rather overestimated the paper's nerve. Re-reading it today it seems, on reflection, to have a woman's touch.

In September 1974, six months after his appointment, it emerged that the Fraud Squad were investigating Lord Brayley's activities as a director of the bottle factory. After a period of reflection Lord Brayley was stripped of office. Then he died. Then the police abandoned their investigations. It was not a succession of events likely to encourage the Prime Minister to offer some sort of explanation. There must have been about 25,000 reasonably unsuccessful business men with some military experience who might have been appointed to run the Army, and Wilson chose the one who was due to be investigated by the Fraud Squad. There it rests: another classic Wilsonian mystery.

A rather more dramatic embarrassment was served up by another of Wilson's friends, the property developer Sir Eric Miller. Miller, who had been knighted by Wilson in 1970, had spent years courting politicians of both parties. With Lord Brayley, he was one of those suspected of having contributed to Wilson's secret fund. He wanted social prominence as well as influence, and he set out to buy both. He acquired a reputation, well justified, for reckless generosity – to the right people. Nor was he a commercial nonentity, unlike Brayley. He was a property developer, the creator of the Peachey Property Corporation, which made genuine millions. Where Wilson was concerned, Miller sponsored him. He lent him a helicopter during the 1970 election campaign; he was one of those who were only too willing to pay for the leader of the Opposition's increasingly expensive needs. Unfortunately he failed to observe the proper distinction between his own money and that of his shareholders. As long as the property market boomed, it hardly mattered; there was always more money for everyone. But once the property slump arrived the truth became clear enough. As the police moved in on another of Wilson's friends, Miller shot himself behind the locked gates and high walls of his heavily guarded house. He had always wanted to be helpful.

The first of the Secret Service information packs to reach *Private Eye* had come by way of *The Times* in 1974. A reporter on that paper had started to check the allegations, established that they were plausible but then decided that the story would be better handled by *Private Eye*. The period covered was immediately after the war, when the country was going through a severe economic depression. At that time the United Kingdom suffered from a shortage of foreign currency and manufacturing resources. The few people who could get permission to import heavily rationed raw materials or finished goods were almost bound to become millionaires. The necessary licences were issued by the President of the Board of Trade, and from October 1947 to March 1951 that person was Harold Wilson. It was during his term of office that Wilson first met several of the men who were later to support, and to benefit from, his political career. One was Montague Meyer, a major importer of timber from Finland. Another was Joe Kagan, whose family textile firm wished to import cheap clothing material from Eastern Europe. A third was Rudy Sternberg. When Wilson went into Opposition after the 1951 general election, Meyer gave him a consultancy which took him on frequent journeys to Moscow and East European capitals. Kagan and Sternberg, both subsequently made peers by Wilson, were later suspected of having contacts with the KGB. It was a story, even then, on a vast scale, stretching back over thirty years and moving from London to Moscow to East Berlin to Bucharest to Tel Aviv. It would have tested the resources of a national newspaper, and it was well beyond the powers of *Private Eye*, to investigate it as thoroughly as it deserved. But although much of the information sent in was anonymous, it was not unconvincing. Where it could be checked, it rang true.

During the war J. H. Wilson, an Oxford PEP graduate, was reserved to work at the Ministry of Works and, in 1943, was made Director of Economics and Statistics at the Ministry of Fuel & Power. In the same year became Principal Assistant Secretary at the

On becoming a MP in 1945 Wilson was appointed Parlty. Secy. to the Minister of Works whilst   became   to Attlee. In March 1947 Wilson was made Secretary for Overseas Trade;   became   Secretary to the   where he continued until, in Attlee's second government he became   to the   ;meanwhile, in October 1947, Wilson had become President of the Board of Trade, a post he retained until March 1951 when he handed over to Shawcross, who held it until the Attlee government fell six months later. Thus Wilson and   served concurrently for four years or more at the BOT and the   respectively.

There is, of course, more to that seemingly innocent coincidence. Although much older than Wilson,   , too, was an Oxford socialist, an anti-European, and a member of Labour's   set.

For four years wilson had ultimate responsibility for all decisions affecting Britain's overseas trade whilst   had almost ultimate responsibility and was certainly in the critical position in the   / that might support the   , and vice-versa.

. . . .

Postwar Finland, a principal timber exporter, was under Russian control until the signature of its peace treaty with the UK and USSR only one month before Wilson became Secretary for Overseas Trade.

For some time after that Treaty the Finnish-UK trade was still very closely bound up with the Soviet Trade Delegation in London.

The STD in London was from its inception immediately postwar and for many years afterwards the principal cover for Soviet Intelligence agents other than those working directly from the Embassy. Although it had a legitimate trade function - all Soviet trade being conducted through the state organisation - under the guise of trade inquiries such agents were able to travel widely throughout the UK, whilst in foreign embassies in Moscow even bona fide British officials such as Attachés were being strictly limited in their travels. In London, protests to the Foreign Office from the Service Ministries were of no avail and they had to see their own information-gathering more and more severely curtailed whilst those of the USSR here were proliferating, and all went hand-in-hand with the Burgess-McLean-Philby-Blake and no doubt other members of the subverted native pro-Russian spy ring.

engineering products.

For instance, in 1947, the year in which Wilson had
become responsible for all overseas trade, the Rolls Royce
jet engines were the best in the world, far in advance
of anything in Russia or America. In 1947 even within
the RAF such equipment was listed by security grades
and none could be exported to foreign countries without
surmounting two obstacles – the first a security clearance
from the Air Ministry and the second the granting of a
special export licence from the Board of Trade.

Surprising, then, that not just one but two RR engines
– the Nene and the Derwent – were able to be exported to
Russia in 1947, to be copied, incorporated into Russia
engineering know-how, and thereafter manufactured there
without any licence payments coming back to RR. This
give-away not only enabled the Russians to catch up
very rapidly with the superior technology in jets then
possessed by the British, but also enabled her to save
the enormous R & D costs that the British people had
spent in developing such products. It is not known
whether the Russians actually paid for these 'exports'
but even if they did so they paid for only one example
of each engine. What is known is that RR themselves
objected, the Asst. Chief of Air Staff (Intelligence)
objected, other Service Ministries objected – but that
all were over-ruled and that the Board of Trade granted
the necessary licences.

It would be interesting to see the Board of Trade,
Foreign Office and Treasury papers relating to this
particular incident; possibly Rolls Royce documents
are no longer available. Certainly no evidence can be
called from the Russians themselves. Nor – short of
seeing documents long dead, perhaps now destroyed –
will probably anyone discover what and how many other
arrangements were arrived at in those years between
the Board of Trade, the Russian Trade Delegation, and
British traders such as, for instance, timber importers.

All we know for certain is that during those years
the Russian Trade Delegation and its proliferating agents
flourished and expanded, as did the Russian radio station,
until the increasingly gross misuse of it reached such
proportions that at long last even the British government
had to clean it out, massively, and at great danger to
the East-West detente forced upon Russia by her breach
with China. But the years in which its greatest harm

Extracts from one of the documents sent to *Private Eye* in 1974, apparently
by MI5.

As we sorted through this material, we were directed back over the years to the 'Groundnut Scheme', the Lynskey Tribunal, the export to Russia of top-secret Rolls-Royce engines, the Leipzig Trade Fair and the opening of the Soviet Trade Delegation in London – after a quarry whose name changed on every other page. Was it the KGB? Was it the Israeli Intelligence Service? Was it some dark alliance of both? Who was the evil genius? Sir Leslie Plummer, MP (deceased)? Or somebody still alive?

And so we would start again and discover, to our astonishment, that Ian Mikardo, MP, had at one time entered into a business partnership, with a London solicitor called Leslie Paisner, that specialized in East German trade. Mikardo's pair in the House of Commons was, of course, Burnaby Drayson, MP, who worked part-time for Rudy Sternberg, as did Beattie Plummer, Sir Leslie's widow, and Wilfred Owen, MP, who had been required to resign after it was revealed that he had been spying for the Czech government, or at least thought he had. Then hardly had we accustomed ourselves to the chilly surroundings of Czech espionage than we were back in the steaming heat of a groundnut plantation somewhere in Tanganyika. And who was that over there, at the edge of the clearing, buying up all the timber that had been felled to make way for the groundnut bushes? Why, if it wasn't our old friend, Montague Meyer.

So what? That, unfortunately, was the one question that we never were able to answer. Just as we were deciding that the whole story was a chimera, through the post would come yet another photostat, this time, perhaps, a copy of what purported to be Edward Short's Swiss bank statement, for December 1972, showing an opening balance of 162,012.05 Swiss francs and a closing balance of 163,528.95. The account had been opened on 1 May 1971 – we had photostat confirmation of that too – but what did it portray and who on earth had posted it to us?

Short, a Newcastle MP, was at that time busily explaining why he had been in the habit of receiving bundles of banknotes from T. Dan Smith, the 'city boss' of Newcastle, corrupter of politicians and civil servants and one-time business partner of Eric Levine.

The correspondence between T. Dan Smith and Short was published at Smith's trial for corruption. As reported in the *Daily Telegraph*, it read as follows:

Dear Ted, I want to show my appreciation of the work you have done on behalf of the firm and I suggest you accept a retainer from me of £500 which would be a strictly confidential matter between us. We can discuss this the next time we meet.

In his reply from the House of Commons Mr Short wrote:

Dear Dan, Thank you for your TDS/JB OS/1 dated 16th January. It is very kind of you to make this offer and provided it can be kept a confidential matter between the two of us I would be pleased to accept it. Of course any help I have been able to give, or will give in the future, is quite unconnected with this and is out of my regard for you personally and for the magnificent job you are doing in the North. Kindest regards.

The report of the cross-examination of Mr Smith continued in this manner:

Mr Potts asked Smith if he was sure the payment was £500.

Smith replied: '*I believe it was £500, although I have obviously seen Mr Short's statement in the Press and he says it was £250.*'

Mr Potts: What method of payment did you adopt? – *I'm speaking from memory. I believe it was in cash and that the cash entry was in the books.*

Cash, Mr Smith? – *I believe so.*

Pound notes? – *I believe so.*

Did you put some pound notes in the post and send them to Patterdale Gardens or the House of Commons? – *I rather think Mr Kirkup* [Smith's chief accountant] *in fact delivered the money to Mr Short, but no doubt the books would show that. It was a recorded transaction to the best of my knowledge.*

Mr Potts asked what Mr Short had done to justify the payment. Smith replied: 'Mr Short had arranged for meetings in the House of Commons with people in industry and commerce. In the main for myself because we were doing a public relations contract for Peterlee which had been up to that time not very successful in securing industry for the area. He assisted in that work and as the rule in the House was that we could not pay for a meal or a drink or anything, Mr Short was out of pocket. That was what he had done and that was why the payment was proposed.'

Mr Smith then said that he thought Mr Short's annual parliamentary salary at this time amounted to about £1,500. The Swiss bank account showed a credit balance nine years later of nearly £30,000. And for at least six of those years there had been in force extremely strict exchange controls that prohibited the export of sterling. The jigsaw became more and more complicated; many of the pieces interlocked, but no final pattern emerged. As for the source of the photostats of Short's bank account, it seemed quite possible at the time that this may have been the Metropolitan Police.* When an investigation was being blocked or when they were looking for more evidence, the police sometimes found it useful to leak information to *Private Eye* in the hope that publication might assist progress. It was a tactic the police were later to use in the prosecution of a senior civil servant for sexual offences.

* Peter Wright, the former MI5 officer and author of *Spycatcher*, has since stated that this document was a forgery circulated by dissident, right-wing officers of MI5 for political reasons.

At least two of Wilson's peculiar friends did eventually emerge from the shadows. Joe Kagan was questioned by the police about tax and currency offences in connection with his Gannex firm. He took refuge in Israel with his secretary. The Israeli police undertook to inform Interpol of his movements, and in due course he returned to England to be tried for theft and false accounting, found guilty and imprisoned. Later it emerged that, at a time when he had the entrée to 10 Downing Street, Kagan was also on friendly terms with Vaygauskas, the K G B station chief in the London Embassy, a man he had first met in Lithuania before the war. Another deafening silence greeted this revelation.

Sir Rudy Sternberg, Lord Plurenden, died in 1980; after his death it emerged that he too had been under suspicion at the Security Service for years. It was thought that he had used his thriving business with importers and exporters in East Germany and Romania as a cover for intelligence activities. It was the presence of suspected Eastern Bloc agents so close to the Prime Minister that had led Sir Martin Furnival Jones, the Director of MI5 to order an investigation of Wilson in 1971, after the C I A had reported that a Russian source had identified him as an agent. In 1974 certain of the MI5 officers involved in the original investigation, according to Peter Wright in *Spycatcher*, started acting on their own initiative. Some of the documents they released reached *Private Eye*, but that paper's investigations ground to a halt for lack of corroborative evidence. The paper is frequently accused of failing to check its stories. Here was a case where the failure of its inquiries caused it to keep silence. We were unable to discover whether or not the K G B had infiltrated Downing Street.

Nor did the police investigation, carried out in the opposite direction, away from Wilson rather than towards him, bear any fruit. The officer leading it was Detective

Chief Superintendent Roy Ranson. He was able to confirm that the tax papers had disappeared but could not confirm the existence of a 'dirty tricks department'. But some members of his team came to know a surprising amount about the social lives of Lord Kagan, Lord Plurenden and even Sir Eric Miller. The relevance of this world to the murder of Lord Lucan was to emerge only later, after the grotesque game of consequences had advanced several more stages.

CHAPTER EIGHT

The Human Time Bomb

Anyone who gets involved in a scrap between Jimmy Goldsmith and *Private Eye* can expect to be hit by flying glass.

W. F. Deedes

In 1973 Marjorie Halls, a civil servant working in the Lord Chancellor's department, sued the Treasury for £50,000. She alleged that her husband, Michael, who had died of a heart attack while he was principal private secretary to Harold Wilson, had been under intolerable strain brought about by the unusual working conditions at 10 Downing Street. Mrs Halls blamed her husband's death on the tension and tantrums inflicted on Michael Halls by Marcia Williams. Mrs Williams was not a civil servant. She worked for the Labour Party as Harold Wilson's political secretary. There could be no more eloquent tribute to the power exercised by Mrs Williams than Mrs Halls's action.

There have been political advisers at No. 10 for many years, and their relationship with the senior civil servants has frequently been tricky. Mrs Williams was probably the most forceful political adviser ever to arrive there. She was also one of the ablest. She gave Wilson the self-confidence and boldness which he frequently lacked, not least when defending her own position. One of her early battles was over 'positive vetting' (security clearance). This was a routine procedure for everyone coming into senior positions of government, but Mrs Williams, for some reason, flatly refused to undergo the procedure, and, with Wilson's support, she was exempted. He argued that she was concerned solely with the party political side of the job and would have no access to official papers. In fact, she did see official papers – even papers classified as 'secret' and 'top secret' – on domestic subjects, but not classified defence or foreign-policy papers. This careful compromise was worked out between Wilson and Derek Mitchell, his original principal private secretary. After limiting Mrs Williams's power, Mitchell lost his job. He was moved from the Prime Minister's office to the Department of Economic Affairs. He was the first senior civil servant who had failed to realize that when he was defying Marcia Williams, he was defying the Prime Minister. After Mr Mitchell's departure the compromise became fairly meaningless, since under Michael Halls, who was described as a 'more pliant character', Mrs Williams saw the minutes of Cabinet committee meetings at which secret foreign and defence papers were discussed. Her feud with Derek Mitchell continued throughout the rest of his career, and it was widely thought that, but for Mrs Williams's opposition, he would have become head of the Civil Service Department at the Treasury in 1974. But though Mrs Williams had her victory over Derek Mitchell, she made enduring enemies within MI5 by refusing to undergo positive vetting.

This, then, was the official world to which Wilson and Mrs Williams returned after the 1974 general election.

Almost immediately the MI5 papers started to reach *Private Eye*, Wilson alleged that a 'dirty tricks department' had stolen his tax papers, and *Private Eye* first drew attention to the extraordinary influence of the Prime Minister's political secretary. It was then too that Douglas Hurd, MP, who as political secretary to Edward Heath in the previous Tory administration would have learned about Mrs Williams's lack of security clearance between 1964 and 1970, asked the following questions in the House of Commons. They were reported in Hansard as follows.

6 MAY 1974   *Oral Answers*

Political Advisers (Security Vetting)

38. **Mr. Hurd** asked the Minister for the Civil Service in which Departments political advisers appointed since 1st March 1974 have so far completed the security vetting procedures appropriate to their functions.

Mr. Robert Sheldon: This is a matter for the Minister in charge of the Departments concerned, but I can assure the hon. Member that the appropriate procedures are being followed in each case.

Mr. Hurd: The hon. Gentleman will know that this Question was transferred to him by the Prime Minister. May we have an assurance covering No. 10 Downing Street, the Foreign Office and the home Civil Service that in no case do political advisers have access to highly classified papers or highly classified information until the appropriate procedures are satisfactorily completed?

Mr. Sheldon: It is the long-standing practice not to comment on the application of security procedures in these cases, but I assure the hon. Gentleman that the procedure which has prevailed in the past is being carried out now.

Asked later what his slightly enigmatic queries might concern, he said that he was 'just putting down a marker'. In

1976, after two years in power, with little warning and for no clear reason, Harold Wilson resigned. Marcia Williams's reign was over.

It would not have been in character for Mrs Williams to go down without a fight, and in July 1975 she attended a dinner party given by David Frost at which she met Jimmy Goldsmith. By then, following the unwelcome attention of *Private Eye* which, with the help of MI5, had been documenting the influence she exercised over Wilson, she had become Lady Falkender. (Wilson's instant reaction to any criticism of Marcia was to defend her. At this stage in her career he had decided that only a life peerage could compensate the hurt to her feelings.) The meeting between Goldsmith and Lady Falkender was to change the course of his life. She became a friend of his and of Annabel Birley, and Goldsmith apparently took the view that she had been wronged by the magazine. He did nothing at that time. But the fuse had been set. He just sat there ticking. Then came the scuffle on the steps of the church in Farm Street after Dominick Elwes's memorial service, which encouraged *Private Eye* to publish an account of the aftermath of the murder of Sandra Rivett and the tensions which had grown up within the circle of Lord Lucan's friends. Much of this article was devoted to the growing importance of Jimmy Goldsmith, and the paper unwittingly libelled Goldsmith by repeating an error which had previously been made in both the *Sunday Times* and the *Daily Express* and stating that he had been present at the lunch that John Aspinall gave on the day after Lucan's disappearance.

Goldsmith was abroad when the article appeared and at first decided to ignore it. But, on returning to England, he was entertained by Paul Johnson, an old adversary of the magazine, and was advised to 'throw the book at *Private*

Eye'.* Goldsmith, who loved being the centre of attention almost as much as he loved flamboyant gestures, was tempted by this suggestion. The same day he went to dinner at David Frost's house. Once again Lady Falkender was a fellow guest, and once again those present urged Jimmy on. It seemed that Marcia had decided to detonate him. He needed no further encouragement. Within three days he had issued sixty-three libel writs and had commenced proceedings for criminal libel.

At first *Private Eye* was baffled by the vigour of Goldsmith's response. Journalism is a hit-and-miss affair. The article about Marcia Williams, which was of far greater 'importance', had provoked little reaction. You can spend years stirring up as much trouble as possible and get no more than a couple of letters marked 'Not for publication' in reply. Then one day the roof falls in. Initially, *Private Eye* wondered whether, in reawakening interest in Lord Lucan, they had increased the likelihood that he would be discovered. Then a theory developed that Goldsmith wished to stop further inquiries into his attempts to patch up the Slater Walker empire. The fact seems to have been that, in causing offence to both Jimmy Goldsmith and Marcia Williams, the *Eye* had given two powerful people, who were supremely well equipped to defend themselves, reason to form an aggressive alliance. It was an alliance which would have caused Lucan, with his rigid views on the 'pre-revolutionary situation', to twitch.

Over the course of the following twelve months Goldsmith would bring a total of nine separate actions, involving the issue of more than 100 writs, and his litigation would illustrate the majestic range of weapons avail-

* For Goldsmith's original motives I have relied on the biography by Geoffrey Wansell, *Sir James Goldsmith: The Man and the Myth*. At the time of writing this book Mr Wansell was employed by Goldsmith on *Now!* magazine.

able to a man who, for whatever reason, was attempting to restrict free publication. Four of the actions were straightforward civil libel actions arising from reports about Goldsmith personally, or his business associates, or his companies. Over one of these matters he also brought a criminal libel prosecution against the editor and a contributor. In a sixth action he attempted to place the magazine under injunction not to write about him or his lawyer until the criminal hearing was over. Two more actions were brought to commit to prison the editor and another contributor for contempt of court. And the ninth case involved attempts by the magazine to prevent Goldsmith from joining seventeen individual newsagents to the libel suits.

The battle lasted from January 1976 to May 1977, with the advantage periodically shifting from one side to the other. Of the nine matters that came up for some sort of judicial decision, five, including the most important, eventually went to Goldsmith, four to the magazine. Mounting his white charger, Goldsmith rode forth in defence of Lady Falkender. Onward to glory, a political career and his own national newspaper! He never apparently grasped the irony in his other stated motive, that in silencing *Private Eye* he would be 'destroying a conspiracy of Marxists and trendies who were poisoning the well of public truth'. He was, in fact, effectively silencing the only newspaper which might have made some headway with the MI5 allegations. And one of the chief beneficiaries of *Private Eye*'s silence on this subject was Lord Kagan, an old and dear friend of Marcia Williams.

The Goldsmith criminal libel case has always been presented as a private case in contrast to the great political criminal libel cases of the past. But there were some reasons for seeing it as a political prosecution in the old tradition.

On 17 May there came the first hint that Goldsmith had supporters in high places who were not afraid to show their partiality. The Labour MP for Lambeth Central, Marcus Lipton, who had earlier commented on a possible conspiracy among Lord Lucan's friends, urged that proceedings for criminal libel should be undertaken only by the Director of Public Prosecutions (DPP). He was supported in the House of Commons by the Labour MP for Luton West, Brian Sedgemore, who said that no public purpose was served by bringing into the public domain 'the private squabbles between fringe bankers and satirical magazines'. Mr Sedgemore claimed that the criminal libel law was 'an affront to the Bill of Rights and a totally unnecessary invasion of the liberty of the individual and freedom of the Press'. A third Labour MP, Max Madden, said that the use of criminal libel proceedings could be 'embraced by Godfatherlike figures in the City and big business to silence the Press'. To all this the Labour Attorney-General, Sam Silkin, could only reply that he had not given any advice to the DPP over these proceedings. However, he had discussed with the Director both the proceedings and the suggestion that they should be taken over. They had agreed that the public interest did not require the DPP to intervene. So Goldsmith had nothing to fear from that direction.

The Attorney-General had declined to intervene on a Monday. Goldsmith's application for a blanket injunction protecting him from being mentioned in *Private Eye* was heard on the Tuesday. On the Wednesday there came another development. The *Daily Express* led its front page with the headline 'IT'S LORD GOLDSMITH'. The story beneath stated as a fact that in his Resignation Honours List Harold Wilson had recommended Goldsmith for a life peerage. No authority was given for this astonishing development, but the *Express* had no doubts about it and had good reason to believe it. Their source was in fact Peter Jay, son-in-law of James Callaghan, the incoming Prime Minister. Callaghan had been appalled when he saw Wilson's Resignation Honours List, which he correctly foresaw would cause uproar in the Labour Party. He suspected, as did many others, that it had been drawn up not by Wilson but by Lady Falkender. (The Press dubbed it the 'Lavender list' because it had been drafted by Lady Falkender on her lavender-coloured notepaper.) Goldsmith's name was the most appropriate choice for a leak, since he was known to be bitterly hostile to socialism, to be a supporter of the Tory Party and to have no outstanding record of public service. The *Evening Standard*, the *Express*'s sister paper, followed up the story with a report that Goldsmith had twice been 'spotted' lunching with Lady Falkender. One of his friends was quoted as saying, 'He is a violent Tory who regards the socialists as enemies.'

Mr Callaghan's ploy was partly successful. When the list was announced, a week later, Goldsmith had been made a knight but not presented with a seat in the House of Lords. (It was probably, in retrospect, a fatal alteration from *Private Eye*'s point of view. Had Goldsmith been given his 'platform', a seat in the Lords, and come under consequent establishment pressure to behave in a more conventional way, he might well have decided to drop his actions against *Private Eye*.) The rest of the list was in itself enough to provoke the row Callaghan had sought to avoid. Ferdinand Mount, writing in the *Daily Mail*, said that Wilson had 'now managed to debase the peerage almost as devastatingly as he had debased the coinage. The latest weird assortment – a gambling crony of Lord Lucan, a mac manufacturer, Mike Yarwood and a couple of showbiz moguls – would do nicely as a jury for the Miss World contest.' Wilson, said Mount, had turned the House of Lords into a 'freak show'. By an extra twist of fate, Lord Lucan's disappearance had led to one of his friends playing a starring role in an Honours List which effectively heralded the end of the socialist government.

The names which caused all this trouble included those of Sir Joseph Kagan (later imprisoned), who became a peer, Edward Short (accused of accepting bribes), who became a Companion of Honour, and Eric Miller (later accused of fraud), who was knighted. No mention was made of the fact that three of those honoured had contributed to Wilson's secret fund in Opposition. Lady Falkender's touch was also shown by the presence of her sister, Peggy Field, who received the OBE. Miss Field had first come to public attention when it was discovered that she had made hundreds of thousands of pounds from dealing in derelict land near Wilson's Liverpool constituency through a company which had conducted some of its business from Wilson's parliamentary office. Lord Kagan and Sir Eric Miller were not the only people on the list who were subsequently of interest to the police. Even one of the showbiz figures, the actor Sir Stanley Baker, was later found to be associated with criminals.

The *Daily Mail* reported that the publication of the list 'followed the completion of an investigation by Sir Philip Allan, the head of the Civil Service, into well-informed leaks about its contents . . . Efforts to trace the leak have failed and Mr Callaghan is unlikely to take any further action.' That, in the circumstances, was not very surprising.

In the House of Commons 105 Labour MPs demanded that the Labour Party disown the list and dissociate itself from 'the inclusion of those we regard as symbolic of the less acceptable face of capitalism'. This was presumably a reference to Sir James Goldsmith and possibly to his eventual brother-in-law, Sir Max Rayne, a property developer and philanthropist, who had become Lord Rayne, among others; but time would show that it was for the light it cast on the less acceptable face of socialism that the list was more remarkable.

*

Throughout the summer of 1976 the battle between Goldsmith and *Private Eye* was fought out. In England the law's delays are a byword, but they hardly seemed to trouble this wealthy litigant, 'the extremely rich man who has shown that he will spare no expense in the employment of counsel', as he was described in one legal opinion. He gave the matter more or less of his attention depending on the rest of his timetable.

Private Eye was advised by James Comyn, QC, an amusing, urbane and gentle Irishman of vast experience, who chain-smoked Sweet Aftons and whose bookcases were punctuated by occasional bottles of Bols, which, judging by the faded yellow of their contents, had not been consulted for years. For the remainder of the proceedings about the only pleasure that was to be found in the legal morass through which *Private Eye* and all involved with it were dragged were the regular meetings held in James Comyn's chambers.

For most people unwillingly involved, litigation is a nightmare of tedium. But there were, during that summer, some memorable moments. One high point was provided by the arrival, in a closed courtroom, of a gorgeous figure in a white suit, white shoes, pink carnation and pink tie. It was Mr Anthony Blond, a director of *Private Eye* and a friend of Goldsmith. Mr Blond had offered his services as a mediator, but even as he erupted into the closed court and proceeded towards the front bench where the leading protagonists sat, his peace mission ground to a halt. His magnificent costume had attracted the attention of everyone in court, even that of the dozing usher. Protesting in vain that he was a party to the action, Mr Blond was led from the room. It was another of history's countless might-have-beens. Then there was the occasion at Bow Street Magistrates' Court, before the Chief Metropolitan Magistrate, Mr Kenneth Baraclough, where the entertainment was provided by Sir James Goldsmith in the witness box. Stimulated by the skilful encouragement of James Comyn, QC, he put on a virtuoso performance. Geoffrey Wansell described the scene as follows:

> To the surprise of some who packed the courtroom, Goldsmith seemed remarkably agitated. He paced up and down the small witness box while presenting his evidence, gesticulating as he always did, occasionally bringing his fist down hard on the rail around him to give emphasis. He was hardly an orthodox witness. Yet it was not a calculated performance. He had always been prone to pace when he was excited, just as he had a tendency to bite his handkerchief, and he had always waved his arms to make a point. An astonished magistrate asked him if he would mind behaving 'a little less theatrically'. Rather taken aback, the French-born Jimmy Goldsmith replied, 'I am sorry, I find it difficult to keep still.'

Ten days later came the 'dustbins case'. During this case it emerged that Goldsmith (who had once called *Private Eye*'s contributors 'scavengers') had employed private detectives to rake through the contents of the magazine's dustbins in order to compile a list of contributors. In order to avoid a charge of theft, Goldsmith's men had photocopied any interesting items and then returned them to the dustbins. The list of *Private Eye*'s contributors that Goldsmith was able to compile by this means was then circulated among his friends. Even Harold Wilson, in a frisky moment, offered it to anyone who was interested. One sees here an unusual image – Goldsmith returning triumphantly from his raid on the dustbins bearing the list of contributors, the tycoon in the role of Labrador carrying a stick.

But such moments were all too scarce as the great financier attempted to nail down his irritating little opponent. First Goldsmith sued *Private Eye* for three libels.

Then he prosecuted it for criminal libel. Then he sued seventeen newsagents for libelling him by selling the magazine. Then he sought an injunction against the magazine, its editor and five independent contributors with wide access to other papers from 'writing, speaking, printing, publishing, distributing or circulating', or causing or permitting those things to be done, 'any words or any pictures or visual images or any matters whatsoever' referring to Goldsmith or 'tending to disparage or cast doubt on the private or professional honesty or integrity of his lawyer or any member of his firm'. (The lawyer in question, Mr Eric Levine, had also been mentioned in one of the articles complained of.) This injunction was denied him on the grounds, not surprising, that it was too wide. Then Goldsmith sought to commit the editor, Richard Ingrams, to prison for contempt of court. Then he sought to sequester the paper's assets, which would have closed it down.

When his legal assault flagged, Goldsmith opened a propaganda offensive. He started to telephone Fleet Street editors and to make 'serious allegations' against various journalists. Two of these, Michael Gillard and Philip Knightley, responded by suing him for libel.

By the end of 1976 even the rich variety of English adversarial procedures was almost exhausted. Two of the cases had reached the House of Lords, and Goldsmith was left with no more than his four civil libel actions and the two cases involving the most important principles of Press freedom: the newsagents' case and the criminal libel prosecution. His writs and summonses had engaged the attention of two magistrates, one High Court master and seventeen judges. Seven more judges would be needed before he was done.

One has to remind oneself that, strange as it might seem, Goldsmith's underlying purpose, throughout this difficult period in his life, was to protect his reputation, secure a position in British public life and purchase a national newspaper. In some respects his handling of the Press was adept. Those leaving the High Court after he had lost one case were handed a press release, hastily typed but perfectly clear, setting out Goldsmith's litigious campaign over the forthcoming weeks in the light of the decision that had been announced only minutes before. At what he judged appropriate moments Sir James also issued 'open letters' to the Press Council or wrote sharply phrased letters to *The Times*.

> Sir [he wrote on 29 April], Lord Shawcross states that he believes passionately in the freedom of the press. So do I. Those who endanger the freedom of the press are those who abuse it.
>
> > Yours truly,
> > James Goldsmith

This particular contribution was capped by Christopher Logue, poet, warrior, ex-jailbird, movie star, translator of Homer and veteran contributor to *Private Eye*. Logue stood Goldsmith's text on its head by altering one word in the last sentence.

> Sir, Mr James Goldsmith states that he believes passionately in the freedom of the press. So do I. Those who endanger the freedom of the press are those who abuse me.
>
> > Yours truly,
> > Christopher Logue

There was another occasion when Goldsmith was wrongfooted in *The Times*, this time by the sub-editor working on the letters column. Writing to complain about *The Times*'s coverage of one of his court appearances, Goldsmith ended his letter: 'You really must do better, my dear Sir, otherwise I might be forced, after all, to buy *The*

Times.' The Times sub merely headed the letter 'Caveat Vendor'.

Then came an exchange of correspondence that cast a clear light on the private values of the Clermont circle. In November 1978 the following letter appeared in *The Times*.

A question of privacy

Sir, Please accept my apologies for referring, in your columns, to an article published today (November 17) in the William Hickey section of the *Daily Express*. I do so because it touches on matters of more general interest.

The article refers to the marriage of Lady Annabel Vane Tempest Stewart and myself which took place yesterday in Paris. Let me explain why we chose Paris. When a middle-aged couple who have shared their lives for the past fourteen years are able to marry it is appropriate that they should choose to do so with the dignity of silence. That is still possible in Paris because not only is there respect for personal privacy but such privacy is protected by law. The *Daily Express* journalist chose to follow Lady Annabel to Paris and to break this law. Therefore I carried out a 'citizen's arrest' of the journalist and disarmed his camera.

Two points of principle arise:

(1) When British journalists travel abroad to democratic and friendly countries should they not respect the laws of such countries?

(2) Is it not time that our legislators finally pluck up the courage to introduce legislation to this country which will protect personal privacy from the abuses of a commercial press which has now become a national disgrace? When their representatives talk of freedom of the press they mean not freedom but licence and permissiveness.

However I would be ungrateful if I were to finish this letter without thanking the *Daily Express* for a wonderful wedding present – the legal opportunity to 'manhandle' a representative of its gossip column.

> Yours faithfully,
> James Goldsmith

There was an unexpected reply to this letter from the *Daily Express* reporter who had been one of those involved.

Sir, Sir James Goldsmith in his letter (November 18) makes one or two foolhardy comments in his review of my reporting of his wedding in Paris.

Firstly, I broke no law in following Sir James's wife Lady Annabel to Paris, I made one brief and perfectly legitimate approach to her – in London – and once in France scrupulously avoided speaking to her. I am as aware of French law as Sir James.

The 'citizen's arrest' to which Sir James refers was, in fact, illegal. When my photographer was taking pictures of the couple in the street, there were several French police at Sir James's disposal standing within calling distance.

Sir James ignored them, and with the help of an aide grabbed the photographer and bundled him inside the offices of Générale Occidentale. There, with the help of several employees, Sir James broke the photographer's camera, broke his spectacles, bruised his ribs and skinned his knuckles. Then, while the photographer was still being held, Sir James 'escaped' in a cowardly fashion.

It seems extraordinary that a man of Sir James's position should then admit to being pleased to engage himself in a public brawl on his wedding day.

Greater minds than mine have already debated the laws of press freedom in these columns and I do not propose to run through the arguments again. But there can be no doubt that it is of legitimate interest when a man like Sir James, who has expressed a desire to enter public life, chooses to alter his marital status. He has made no secret in the past of being married to a Frenchwoman while fathering the children of his English mistress.

Finally, let there be no mistake about the *Daily Express*'s coverage of Sir James's wedding. There was no hole-in-the-corner subterfuge. The couple were aware of my presence in Paris. I deliberately kept out of their way so as not to ruin what should have been a happy day.

Indeed, my only contact was to send Lady Annabel two
dozen roses. I hope she enjoyed them.

> Yours faithfully,
> Christopher Wilson,
> William Hickey Column,
> *Daily Express*

The world of honour, privilege and action lived on, if only
in Paris. And Goldsmith, who had started adult life by
being threatened with a horsewhip, had graduated to
wielding one.

The battle between Goldsmith and *Private Eye* was the last
act of an outgoing Labour administration which had waged
a steady campaign against the Press. In England, politics
are frequently disguised as something else – soap opera,
gossip, a clash of personalities, anything will do as long as
it extols the individual and distracts attention from the
discussion of ideas. Harold Wilson's associates had become
increasingly hostile to the Press, and to television, ever
since things had first started to go wrong for him in 1967.
Under his leadership a string of measures had been
introduced, all of which tended to restrict freedom to
comment. The copyright laws had been extended in favour
of commercial secrecy; the Press for the first time had been
prevented by law from reporting criminal convictions; Press
reporting of criminal trials was progressively restricted;
and the deliberations of the Cabinet were made even more
secret. In these measures the Labour government was
supported by a wider prejudice against disclosure. It is a
particularly English phenomenon that when the bankruptcy
laws assist, by good fortune, in the uncovering of a
national network of public corruption (as happened in the
Poulson case) there should be immediate pressure, inside
and outside Parliament, to *change the bankruptcy laws*.

There is more than one way of controlling a free Press.

The Conservatives own it. But a Labour government has to find other means of bringing it to heel. In his battle against *Private Eye* Goldsmith was inspired by Labour tacticians, and for the Press the results of those tactical decisions were serious. Labour consistently uses the law to assert its party interests above the public's right to know what is going on in government. It was a Labour government that set up the Press Council and instituted both the post-war Royal Commissions on the Press. If, as in this case, the Labour government did not have to initiate anti-Press litigation itself, but merely refused to intervene in other people's initiatives, then so much the better for Labour. There was nothing necessarily venal, the party would argue, about a Labour Attorney-General interpreting the public interest to coincide with the interests of the Labour Party. His inactivity could be explained as simply as that.

A week after the *Private Eye* criminal libel case was finally settled, the *Daily Mail* published serious allegations about bribery in the nationalized British car industry. The evidence included a letter which turned out to be a forgery. The immediate reaction of one Labour Member of Parliament, Brian Sedgemore, was to urge the Attorney-General to prosecute the editor of the *Daily Mail* for criminal libel. One year earlier, in reference to the Goldsmith prosecution, the same MP had said: 'The criminal libel law is an affront to the Bill of Rights and a totally unnecessary invasion of the liberty of the individual and freedom of the Press.'

As soon as the freedom of the Press is entrusted to politicians it becomes a very fragile plant.

Just as the prosecution of *Private Eye* can be seen as a political prosecution, inspired by Wilson and Lady Falkender and presided over by Sam Silkin, so the defence of the paper can be seen as a political defence. Mr Justice

Donaldson was known to have been sympathetic to the Conservatives. Lord Shawcross had little reason to admire Harold Wilson. And the magazine was finally removed from the hook by the intervention of some of the most Conservative interests in Fleet Street. But England is an old country with a talent for dissimulation. Its political battles do not have to be presented as such.

Long after the struggle with *Private Eye* was over, Goldsmith presented the Media Committee of the Conservative Party with a 'statement' entitled 'Communist Propaganda Apparatus and Other Threats to the Media'. It was a document which would have startled Lord Lucan less than Sir James's appearance in the 'Lavender list'. The statement outlined various Soviet attempts to orchestrate a world propaganda campaign. It went on to suggest that many British journalists were unwitting dupes of such campaigns and ended by demanding new laws which would 'make it necessary for all journalists, or anyone else receiving payments and inducements from a foreign government, to register as an agent of that country'.* It also demanded that 'the media and those who are involved with it should disclose the sources of their funds'.

Commenting on Goldsmith's obsession with communist infiltration of the media, the then editor of the *Daily Telegraph*, W. F. Deedes (not a noted fellow traveller), wrote:

> Goldsmith himself takes particular exception to *Private Eye*'s use of journalists – particularly City journalists – who write in other newspapers. He calls it a 'symbiotic relationship' and believes it to be in the nature of a dangerous conspiracy.
>
> Moonlighting for *Private Eye* by journalists on other staffs strikes me as offside, to be frowned on, disciplined

---

* Sir James himself can theoretically claim the protection of four countries: Britain, France, the United States and Israel.

even. On the other hand no power on earth can stop
journalists on different newspapers from gossiping over a
glass and to call that 'incestuous' conduct is plain silly . . .
Goldsmith is still very much at war with his critics and is
just now engaged in an acrimonious exchange with the
Press Council about its failure to do his bidding.

Goldsmith wants the Council to declare its principles on
certain matters. One is payment to witnesses in criminal
prosecutions. Fair enough. Another, more oddly, is
'disclosure by journalists and the media in general of
payments and other inducements received from foreign
countries'. A third, harking back to the symbiotic
relationship point, is 'disclosure by journalists of conflicts
of interest'.

So far the Press Council has returned a dusty answer.
Goldsmith has circulated some of the correspondence to 120
M Ps 'who have written to Sir James Goldsmith showing
sympathy and interest in the points raised by him
concerning the Press Council'.

Bluntly, what Goldsmith appears to be doing is to
mix matters which are particularly obnoxious to him with
more general matters on which there is genuine public
concern (e.g. payment of witnesses) and to seek
influential support for a crusade on the package. If I do
him an injustice here, I shall be the first to hear about it.

He is a man of exemplary determination. As a
publisher he carries some extra weight. He scents,
perhaps, that here and there (most notably in the T U C
and, most ironically, on the left) there is a mood which
would gladly go along with moves to circumscribe by
codes of conduct (outside the courts) the capacity of
newspapers to attack, criticize and disclose – sometimes
unfairly, 'to tell lies' is how Goldsmith would put it.

Self-interest apart, Goldsmith would argue, I suspect,
that our present national state is too fragile, too perilous,
to permit self-indulgent scavenging by the news media.
Plenty of people would trot along with that. His crusade

is by no means derisory. He may have some success. That disturbs me.

Goldsmith's new publication has had more than its share of advice from smug contemporaries. I venture to offer one piece more to the proprietor himself. Let him turn up Alexis de Tocqueville's 'Democracy in America', his essay on the Press, and consider this passage:

> So, where the Press is concerned, there is not in reality any middle path between licence and servitude. To cull the inestimable benefits assured by freedom of the Press, it is necessary to put up with the inevitable evils springing therefrom.
>
> The wish to enjoy the former and avoid the latter is to indulge in one of those illusions with which sick nations soothe themselves when, weary of struggle and exhausted by exertion, they seek means to allow hostile opinions and contradictory principles to exist together at the same time.

As a publisher of promise, he really ought to have that in a neat little frame somewhere on his desk.

Goldsmith won his battle against *Private Eye*, but it was a Pyrrhic victory. He never managed to buy a national newspaper. (*Caveat vendor.*) Instead he started his own. It was called *Now!* magazine, and it closed down after nineteen months with losses put at £6 million. The eighty journalists employed by Goldsmith were given generous pay-offs. It was just three months after their proprietor had presented his statement on the media to the House of Commons.

There were many ironies in the battle between Goldsmith and *Private Eye*. Not the least of them was that the man who embroiled himself in six years of litigation after being urged to avenge a lady who refused to be positively vetted should have ended up by seeing Reds under every bed in Fleet Street.

Private Eye survived his attack and went on to double its

circulation. Goldsmith survived the loss of *Now!* and went on to become richer and richer and richer, not in England but in America. But there were others involved, individual 'elements of the urban biomass', who had been badly cut by the flying glass. The shade of Lord Lucan was still rattling its chains.

CHAPTER NINE

The Elusive Mr Addey

When the sands are all dry, he is gay as a lark,
And will talk in contemptuous tones of the Shark,
But, when the tide's high and sharks are around,
His voice has a timid and tremulous sound.

from Lewis Carroll, Alice in Wonderland

Lord Lucan's wife had displeased him; he decided that she must be killed, but it was Mrs Rivett who died. The *Sunday Times Magazine* intruded on the private grief of Lucan's friends, but it was Dominick Elwes, one of their own circle, who was made the scapegoat and hounded to his death. Sir James Goldsmith objected to *Private Eye*'s description of Elwes's suicide and threatened to close the magazine, but it was his own magazine which eventually had to close. Time and again a blow intended for one head cracked another. It was as though they were all aimed by a man wielding a bludgeon in the dark.

The sequels to the original crime by now involved other issues of public importance, such as the behaviour of MI5 and the law of criminal libel. But there were further individual disasters in store. The first indication of these came in May 1976, when sensational and self-destructive affidavits were sworn by two prominent professional men, Leslie Paisner and John Addey. Mr Paisner and Mr Addey were very different characters from those previously drawn into the story.

John Addey, a successful City PR man, had for some years been one of the most welcome guests at *Private Eye*'s 'Wednesday lunch'. He was amusing, energetic, well informed and generous with his information. He was always approachable and rarely unable to help with an anecdote or a significant detail. He was regarded, with reason, as a friend of the magazine.

Leslie Paisner, a more considerable figure, was the senior partner in a family firm of solicitors, Paisner & Co., which he had built up into one of the top financial solicitors in London. He was a respected and popular member of the legal community, known to numerous judges and barristers as a man whose ability had made the high reputation of his firm. He had had no previous contact with *Private Eye*. On the only occasion when I met him, he gave a strong impression of being an upright man, a father figure who was proud of his firm, quietly spoken, dignified and reassuring. During about an hour's conversation he told me that when he heard of the criminal libel action he thought it was time to speak out about Goldsmith's solicitor, Eric Levine, a man who had once been one of his partners but who, said Mr Paisner, had left the firm in disgrace. Shortly after speaking to *Private Eye*, Mr Paisner withdrew all the allegations he had made against Eric Levine. In doing so he signed an affidavit of which James Comyn, QC, said when he read it, 'It is one of the most remarkable affidavits I have ever seen. If it ever comes out, Paisner will be ruined.' It did indeed come out and Mr Paisner was ruined. What had happened?

On 21 April, one week after Mr Justice Wien had author-
ized the prosecution for criminal libel, John Addey had, as
was his custom, attended a *Private Eye* lunch and supplied
those present with various stories. On this occasion Addey
chose to offer stories to the discredit of Eric Levine, who
was Goldsmith's solicitor. Subsequently Addey told *Private
Eye* that the source of these stories was Levine's former
employer, Leslie Paisner. For *Private Eye* this seemed to be
a god-sent opportunity. Reeling from the unexpected
ferocity of Goldsmith's attack and the criminal libel prosecution, we were suddenly offered this astonishing information. It was obviously an important story in itself,
but could it also be connected in some way with the
'overkill' of Goldsmith's response?

Addey arranged for a representative from the magazine
to call on Mr Paisner. The representative chosen was
myself. At the meeting Mr Paisner supplied detailed
allegations of criminal behaviour by his former junior
partner. Mr Paisner's decision to talk about a former
partner's misbehaviour was most unusual in any circumstances. None of us knew, at that time, that Mr Paisner
was a former business partner, with Ian Mikardo, MP, in a
firm that specialized in East–West trade, and that he might,
therefore, have had more than a passing interest in the
allegations being circulated by MI5. He himself explained his decision to talk to *Private Eye* by referring to
our success in exposing public corruption, which, he said,
had reached unprecedented levels. Mr Paisner urged that
all his allegations against Eric Levine should be checked
with other parties involved wherever possible, so I went
away and started to check them.

What happened next was that, unknown to *Private Eye*,
John Addey, showing a duplicity for which he was to
become well known, told a business acquaintance who was
in touch with Goldsmith what Paisner had said about

Levine. On 13 May Goldsmith met Mr Paisner, who again made a number of very serious allegations about Mr Levine's conduct before he became Goldsmith's solicitor and while he was still a partner in Paisner's firm. Three days after that meeting Mr Paisner completely changed his story. On 16 May he swore an affidavit that had been typed on a typewriter in Eric Levine's office. This was the document that Mr Comyn said would ruin him, and of which Lord Justice Templeman was later to say that it 'read like a confession from a Moscow show trial'.

I, LESLIE LAZARUS PAISNER, of 73 Harley House, Marylebone Road, London NW 1, Solicitor of the Supreme Court, make oath and say as follows:

1. After Eric Levine left Paisner & Co., the firm of which I am senior partner, in October 1969 I have deliberately on a number of occasions seriously defamed him alleging, among other things that he left the firm as a result of discreditable conduct, he was crooked or dishonest, and that he was unfit to be a solicitor.

2. I have also made other serious allegations attacking Eric Levine's good name and reputation including the following:

(1) That he misappropriated partners' money.

(2) That he participated or was involved in the illegal transfer of funds belonging to the Refson family and that when they claimed title to the funds or the securities represented thereby he denied all knowledge of the transaction.

(3) That he was a business partner of Mr T. Dan Smith and Mr R. Dilleigh and as such was involved in illegal or improper activities.

3. I hereby unequivocally acknowledge that all these statements and allegations were lies and without any foundation whatsoever. They were part of a vicious

vendetta perpetrated by me on Eric Levine. I withdraw
each and every one of them unreservedly. I made these
outrageous allegations against Eric Levine because his
departure from the firm, particularly to join Charles Forte
who was one of my personal friends and clients, was a
major blow to me. Also my relationship with Eric Levine
had been a close one. His departure turned my feelings to
hatred. Despite my attacks against Eric Levine he
prospered. The success of his firm embittered me the more,
particularly when I learnt that the successful Jimmy
Goldsmith had become his client. In his early days he had
been a client of my firm.

4. When John Addey came to see me on 20th April he told
me that a customer of one of his banking clients had lost
£150,000 because of Eric Levine's misconduct and was
considering suing or prosecuting him. He asked me what I
knew about Eric Levine. I saw this as an opportunity,
through Addey's client, to ensure that Eric Levine would
be ruined. I therefore told Addey a pack of lies about him:
that he was a crook, that he had been thrown out of my
firm, that he had participated in illegally transferring money
out of the country for a client and had then
misappropriated it and that I regretted the day I ever met
him. I did this because I hoped this would encourage the
other party to prosecute Eric Levine. This would then have
vindicated what I had been saying over the years about
Eric Levine. John Addey yesterday confessed to me that
all he told me was a pack of lies fabricated to get
information from me about Eric Levine for Private Eye
who were blackmailing him [Addey] and who were
embarked on a campaign of vilification against Eric Levine.

5. Then when Patrick Marnham of Private Eye called me
on 5th May to ask what I knew about Eric Levine I saw
yet another opportunity to bring about Eric Levine's
downfall without being seen to be involved myself. I,
therefore, *repeated to Private Eye* what I told Addey and other
similar seriously damaging statements.

6. All that I told John Addey and Patrick Marnham of Private Eye was a complete pack of lies from beginning to end and without any truth or foundation. I have withdrawn all these statements and allegations.

7. I am deeply ashamed of my conduct. Only now do I fully understand how vindictive it has been and what harm and damage I have caused Eric Levine. I now wish to put an end to the campaign I mounted against Eric Levine and ensure that he suffers no further damage as a result of the lies I have told about him.

This affidavit, sworn on 16 May, remained in Goldsmith's pocket until the date of his application for an injunction to prevent *Private Eye* and five independent journalists* from writing anything, anywhere, about him or his solicitor, Eric Levine, until the verdict in the criminal libel trial. The hearing of Goldsmith's application opened on 5 July before Mr Justice Donaldson, sitting in chambers. At that hearing Mr Paisner's doctor, Dr Nigel Southward, explained what had happened to his patient in the interim.

Dr Southward said that he had been called to see Mr Paisner at the end of May, when he had found his patient, a previously healthy man, suffering from an 'acute anxiety state'. He was mildly confused. Mr Paisner had never suffered from any psychiatric trouble before, but Dr Southward referred him to a psychiatrist, who said that he was probably slowing down mentally. Dr Southward advised him to work less hard and to take a holiday. He took a holiday but it failed to effect a cure. The affidavit he had sworn on 16 May was due to be produced in court on 7 July. Until then it received no publicity. On 6 July Mr Paisner was served with a subpoena and advised that he

---

* Nigel Dempster, Michael Gillard, Auberon Waugh, Richard West and the author.

would have to face cross-examination on his affidavit. This news caused a mental crisis. His doctor was called again and found that Mr Paisner was by now extremely confused and disorientated. 'He looked ill and exhausted . . . He was unable to give a coherent account of himself . . . He kept repeating that he just wanted to go to sleep. Seen again in the morning, he lay motionless in bed and kept saying that he wanted to end it all.' His doctor diagnosed an acute depressive state, which he thought would last about a week. He would be unable to do himself 'a fair degree of justice' while giving evidence before then. The consequence was that Mr Paisner would be unable to come to court.

In cross-examination of Dr Southward, James Comyn, QC, established that Mr Paisner was in practice and had attended his office in the normal way throughout the week. He had also attended a legal consultation after being served with the subpoena. The doctor said that it had been the subpoena which had precipitated his depression and his thoughts of suicide. There was nothing simulated about his mental anguish.

A second affidavit was then provided by another missing witness, John Addey, described as the director of a public relations consultancy. *Private Eye* had served him too with a subpoena. He had taken himself not to his bed but to his travel agent; he was in Italy and so evaded service.

John Addey's affidavit, which had been made out at Sir James Goldsmith's City office two days before Leslie Paisner's, confirmed the latter's. Among other things it said:

> I asked him [Mr Paisner] to tell me his experience of Eric Levine and he asked me why. I told him an American bank was involved, and there was a client of theirs who had been involved in a deal with Levine. Could she deal and trust

him? He told me – in strict confidence and to tell no one.
He said:

1. That Eric Levine had been a partner and he had taken
him as an articled clerk. He was brilliant, should have got
a first, but had liked the bright lights too much.

2. He had taken some £20,000 more from the firm than he
should, and Paisner's partners had recommended he go.
Paisner kept him on. Levine then had involvements with
Refson (for whom with another he had taken £150,000
to Switzerland and, later, when asked for it, had said it
couldn't be handed over, as the original transaction was
illegal, thereby keeping the money).

3. T. Dan Smith, and Dilleigh, where Levine had acted
more as principal than as lawyer.

Why, I asked, did he now act for Goldsmith if he had
such a history? Paisner said: 'Some people need to have a
lawyer like that.'

In addition, Addey's affidavit claimed that Michael Gillard
of *Private Eye* had threatened to expose him as a
homosexual if Addey did not help the magazine.

Evidence of this alleged 'blackmail' was attached to
Addey's affidavit. It was a copy of a memorandum that
had been sent to *Private Eye* some time before and that,
Addey alleged, Michael Gillard had used to put pressure
on him. The memo read as follows:

The rise and fall of John Addey
It is hard times at Wardrobe Chambers for City guide John
Addey.

Apart from firing – or serving protective notice on a dozen
of his executives (they're not sure who is protected) – the
master himself has had to make one or two slimline
gestures.

Gone for instance is his vintage Bentley . . . and his

chauffeur – dear Jeffrey. But then that makes it easier to persuade staff (remaining) to travel by bus and tube.

The Adder's problem is something to do with cash flow.

Earlier this year he was spending £3,000 on a Press party at the City Golf. Then £17,000 doing up the dungeons at Wardrobe Chambers as an executive dining-room suite. Some might have thought it helped keep exhibitions subsidiary – Jaddex – busy until Addey could find a buyer.

Now he's had to part – to Charles Barker – with his advertising, house journal and design dept.

Gone, too, his ambitions, to buy out *Voice and Vision* for a song. To set up a PR – travel to – op. in Cyprus.

Most of the financial clients seem to be tightening their belts. And so we have a slimline Adder.

All he's left with is his executive dining suite, his wine vault in Albany, his imported (£1,000 a time) lions from America.

Finally Addey had made out a second affidavit on 17 May, the day after Paisner's affidavit had been sworn. Again he went to Goldsmith's office to do this. In it he included various details about the dinner with Michael Gillard that had earlier eluded his memory.

The timetable, then, was as follows. On 14 April 1976 Mr Justice Wien astonished the world by giving Goldsmith leave to bring criminal libel proceedings against *Private Eye*. One week later, on 21 April, John Addey attended lunch at *Private Eye*. On the following day he saw Paisner and told him an invented story to the discredit of Eric Levine. Two weeks later I met Paisner. The conversation at this meeting was reported by Michael Gillard to Addey. Some time during the next six days Addey repeated all this confidential information to a colleague of Goldsmith. On 13 May Paisner personally repeated his allegations about Eric Levine to Goldsmith. On the following day Addey signed a statement, an unsworn affidavit, saying that he had lied to Paisner and that he was being blackmailed by *Private Eye*. Two days after that, on a Sunday, Paisner, who was now deprived of his original reason for attacking Levine, swore the affidavit that was to end his professional life. On the next day Addey signed his second statement, another unsworn affidavit, which amplified his first. On that day too the Attorney-General, Sam Silkin, declined to intervene in the criminal libel case. On the day following that, a Tuesday, Goldsmith, armed with these statements, applied for his blanket injunction against *Private Eye* and five of its contributors. The next day the *Daily Express* printed a story saying that Goldsmith was due to get a peerage in Harold Wilson's Resignation Honours List.

By this point the situation had attained an almost Venetian complexity. Leslie Paisner, the senior partner in one of London's leading firms of solicitors, a man past the age of retirement who lived for his work, a man who had spent his life and built his reputation by dispensing wise counsel, advising caution, conducting negotiations and behaving at all times with utter discretion, had apparently, if one were to take his affidavit at face value, become consumed with jealousy because of the relatively slight success of a former junior partner and had set out to destroy this man with a campaign of vile and reckless lies. In doing so he had urged those to whom he was telling these lies to check them thoroughly, thereby exposing himself to the near-certain risk of discovering that he was a dangerous liar.

Alternatively, if you took the attitude to the affidavit shared by James Comyn, QC (now Mr Justice Comyn), Mr Justice Donaldson (now Lord Donaldson, Master of the Rolls) and Lord Justice Templeman (now Lord

Templeman, Lord of Appeal in Ordinary) and regarded
the affidavit as extraordinary, self-destructive and a put-up
job, then it would seem, in the words of Mr Justice
Donaldson, that 'someone had twisted Mr Paisner's arm'.
But who *could* twist the arm of such a senior figure? Mr
Justice Donaldson said that he understood that *Private Eye*
believed that Goldsmith had done it.

The case that Goldsmith's lawyer argued in front of Mr
Justice Donaldson was that Goldsmith should be granted
an injunction in the widest possible terms because *Private
Eye* was using blackmail to promote a campaign of lies
against Goldsmith and his solicitor to persuade them to
drop the criminal libel action. *Private Eye*, in reply, denied
that it was using blackmail and said that it was merely
attempting to continue functioning as a newspaper as well
as defending itself against a novel form of prosecution. Mr
Justice Donaldson, having heard arguments from both
sides, refused to give Goldsmith the injunction he sought.

Mr Paisner never appeared as a witness in court, never
made a public statement and never returned to his practice.
In August 1976 his resignation from the board of Keyser
Ullmann, the merchant bank, on grounds of ill-health was
reported. When he died in 1979 the Chief Rabbi said of him:

> As a Jew, as a lawyer, and simply as a beautiful human
> being, Leslie Paisner had few peers. He was possessed of
> an extraordinary capacity to radiate friendship and kindness,
> lavishing his own wisdom and help on numerous
> communal causes and countless individuals whose lives he
> enriched. His religious piety encompassed a passion for
> moral rectitude and a deep love of Jewish learning and
> tradition. A true nobleman in action and disposition, he
> won the highest accolade of acclaim for his successes in
> deeds, even as he was a source of inspiration for the dignity
> with which he bore suffering and adversity . . . His rich
> legacy will for ever live on.

The *Jewish Chronicle*, in its obituary of Mr Paisner, mentioned his charitable work and his 'magnificent assistance' to Jewish education and to the advancement of religious studies. The Jewish community, then, does not seem to have been unduly impressed by the offences that Mr Paisner alleged against himself in his astonishing affidavit.

So what were Leslie Paisner's true motives for talking so uncharacteristically to *Private Eye*? As both the solicitor for Sir Isaac Wolfson and the business associate of Ian Mikardo, Mr Paisner spanned the political range of Jewish public life, from Marxism to ultra-capitalism. As a benefactor of Zionist causes he would have been well acquainted with men like Sir Samuel Fisher and Sigmund Sternberg, who were both contributors to Harold Wilson's secret fund. What can have been the motive for his reckless and self-destructive attack on Eric Levine? Had he conceived an immoderate but unrequited passion for his brilliant young partner, as may have been hinted at in his affidavit? Was it all just an affair of the heart? It hardly seems likely. Leslie Paisner's downfall is another of the mysterious and unimaginable sequels to the death of Sandra Rivett.

Eric Levine, the object of Leslie Paisner's attack, maintained an overall silence, but he did eventually advance a 'collateral defence', also in the *Jewish Chronicle*. Contributing to a column called 'Open Forum', two months after Mr Paisner's obituary had appeared, Levine wrote:

> Any comment from me on the litigation between Sir James Goldsmith and *Private Eye* would be inappropriate, since I am clearly partisan. One point, however, is worth noting.
>
> Only last week were the true facts of the sadder aspects of the affair revealed in full for the first time in the High Court.* Anyone forming an opinion without knowledge of

---

* A reference to the libel action that Sir James Goldsmith had just won against Michael Gillard.

these facts does himself a disservice. Hillel's advice as to judgement of one's neighbour is particularly apposite . . .

As Jews, we know too well from our long history the damage caused by false reporting . . .

Words are an essential tool of the anti-Semite. They sow the seeds of hatred in the mind. Without that hatred no pogrom could be perpetrated, no final solution promoted . . .

One word of caution. Attack against a person *because* he is a Jew must be distinguished from criticism of a person who happens to be Jewish. We have our sinners, too.

Perhaps more important than all this is how we conduct our own lives. If we expect to be reported on fairly, shouldn't we ourselves don the same mantle when we report on others?

It was surely no hollow recrimination when our rabbis taught that the ornate Second Temple was destroyed by *sinai chinam* – groundless hatred and dissension among the Jews. Would our own communal edifice not benefit from the spirit of *jahavat israel* – love of our fellow Jews?

If we demonstrate our mutual love would we not be better placed to call for vigilance of that quality in the world at large? Would that not make us better Jews and better citizens?

This interesting document bore some stylistic resemblance to the affidavit sworn by Mr Paisner but typed on Mr Levine's typewriter. Its last three paragraphs were a rider to the Chief Rabbi's praise of Mr Paisner. Its reference to *Private Eye* did not represent the first time that Goldsmith or Levine had attempted to justify *Private Eye*'s attack on them as anti-Semitism. With reference to these complaints Chaim Bermant, contributing to the *Jewish Chronicle* under the name of Ben Azai, wrote as follows:

I am glad that the Goldsmith *v. Private Eye* case has been settled out of court.

I am no lover of *Private Eye* – very few people are – but

the trial would probably have killed it and, like anyone who lives by the word, I hate to see any magazine go down. And, in any case, if it had gone down, it might have been replaced by something even worse.

Sir James Goldsmith is a member of a comparatively impecunious branch of a wealthy banking clan. His father was a mere hotel owner; his grandfather a Rothschild-Goldsmid.

The late James de Rothschild was his godfather and, at his behest, Goldsmith went to live in Israel for a while shortly after he left Eton. But he always had an ambition to become a Rothschild in his own right, and Israel, especially during the days of *tzena* (austerity), was not quite the place for it. He returned to Europe, and the rest we know.

His attitude to Judaism has been somewhat ambivalent. He used to go to Upper Berkeley Street on Yom Kippur, when his father was alive, and his first wife, Isabel Patino, was in the course of being converted to Judaism by an Orthodox Beth Din (though he will admit that his own lifestyle is somewhat less than Orthodox, or indeed orthodox) when she died in childbirth.

Yet, apart from an intermittent concern about Israel, Goldsmith was only vaguely aware of his Jewishness until *Private Eye* began what he regarded as a personal vendetta against him. Scratch a semi-Jew and one will discover a full one.

Levine's career as a London solicitor came to a halt after the legislation between Goldsmith and *Private Eye*. He was mentioned in critical terms in two reports compiled by inspectors from the Department of Trade and Industry and was investigated by the Professional Practices Committee of the Law Society on at least two occasions. Following these investigations he was not disciplined, but the firm of Eric Levine & Co. closed down, he vacated his magnificent suite of offices in Berkeley Square and in 1980 he was reported (as was Goldsmith) to be living in New York and 'active' on the Manhattan property market. His current entry in the *Solicitor's Diary* gives no London address.

As for John Addey, he appeared at first to weather the storm. Technically his affidavit had never been sworn, which meant that had he subsequently decided to retract every word in it, he could not have been charged with perjury. He was absent when the hearing opened, on 'urgent business in Italy'. There was a suggestion at one point that the case should be adjourned until he had returned, but it went ahead. By the time it had finished, a few days later, Addey was back in England.

When news of the allegation that Addey had supplied information about his own clients to *Private Eye* got around, one of his clients decided to find another public relations adviser. The chairman of Tesco's said, 'Financial PR is a confidential affair and much of the information involved in it is privileged . . . This last burst of publicity was the last straw.' Addey faced a revolt from his own board of directors, the majority of whom demanded, and received, his resignation from the post of chief executive. Later Addey, who had retained financial control of the company, outfoxed the board and voted himself back. His company continued to operate and he continues to head it today.

Throughout the story Addey seemed prepared to say the first plausible thing that might assist his own position. So two days after signing his unsworn affidavit, which he did quite willingly, according to the Commissioner for Oaths, Addey was summoning Richard Ingrams to his flat in Albany, claiming to have been threatened by Goldsmith and Levine with a criminal libel action and agreeing therefore to provide them with a false affidavit. 'I did not realize they had so much power,' Addey, who was very upset, said to Ingrams. Then he swore Ingrams to secrecy about the meeting and publicly stood by his false affidavit.

Ingrams, despite this, kept his word about the secrecy of
the meeting and did not even mention it in his own
affidavit, although his lawyers urged him to do so. This
gave Addey the opportunity, which he seized at once, to
disclose that the meeting had taken place and to claim that
Ingrams had threatened him at the meeting rather than
that he, Addey, had claimed to have been threatened. The
fact is that if the courts are considering the evidence of a
man who will tell any lie, however damaging, if he thinks
he can get away with it, and if that man avoids coming to
court for cross-examination, then the courts are at the
mercy of the liar, not vice versa.

In 1979 the Department of Trade and Industry published
the report of its inspectors into the affairs of Christopher
Selmes, an asset-stripping property developer. Selmes had
borrowed £20 million from Keyser Ullmann in December
1973 against personal guarantees. A property deal had gone
wrong; Selmes had salted away his assets, and the bank
had released him from his debts for a payment of only
£150,000. During the property deal John Addey had
prepared a press release which, according to the inspectors,
contained allegations of material facts which were simply
not true. 'Mr Addey,' said the inspectors, 'was neither full
nor frank in his evidence to us and knew much more than
he cared to disclose.'*

Despite his performance in the Paisner case Addey was
invited to sit as a Justice of the Peace in London's South
Central Division and was appointed in July 1977. He was
not 'removed' from the bench until June 1978.

Anyone who tried to interpret John Addey's behaviour
throughout these events in a sympathetic light would be
setting himself a difficult task. A moderate summary might
be to say that, emerging from a strong field, Addey

* The report also mentioned evidence provided by Eric Levine, which Mr
Levine himself had subsequently described as 'inaccurate'.

established himself as the least attractive character in the entire story. Nor was his mischief-making finished yet. The list of broken friendships already included Elwes and Goldsmith, Goldsmith and Paisner, Paisner and Addey, and Addey and Gillard. One more nail remained to be driven into the coffin of the last friendship.

Lord Wigg in November 1976. He had become Lord Wigg of the Borough of Dudley in 1967.

Lady Falkender at her desk at No. 10. And (*opposite*) with the Prime Minister, Harold Wilson.

Rudy Sternberg, made Lord Plurenden by Harold Wilson in 1975. After his death in 1978, it was said that he had been a Soviet agent for many years.

Sir Eric Miller, knighted by Harold Wilson in 1976. He committed suicide while his property company was being investigated by the Fraud Squad in 1977.

(*Left*) Lord Brayley, former Army minister, made a peer by Harold Wilson in 1973. He died in 1977 while awaiting trial at the Old Bailey for conspiracy to defraud.

(*Below*) Lord Kagan, made a peer by Harold Wilson in 1976. He was subsequently convicted and sent to prison for offences against the Company Law and Customs regulations.

(*Above*) Sir James Goldsmith, knighted in Harold Wilson's Resignation Honours List in 1976.

(*Opposite*) Lord Glenamara, formerly Edward Short. Once one of Harold Wilson's ministers, he was accused of possessing an illegal Swiss bank account; it has subsequently been revealed that this was the result of a plot by MI5.

Lady Lucan posing with a picture of her husband for the *Daily Mirror* in 1979.

CHAPTER TEN

Playing Leapfrog

One staff officer jumped right over another staff
   officer's back,
And another staff officer jumped right over that other
   staff officer's back,
A third staff officer jumped right over . . ., etc.
   Refrain: They were only playing leapfrog (repeat)
         Song from *Oh, What a Lovely War!*

When the day came for the criminal libel trial in May 1977
and we had to go to No. 1 Court at the Old Bailey and
stand in the dock from which Crippen and William Joyce
were taken to be hanged, though in our case it was to be
formally acquitted, I felt very glad that the trial had not
gone ahead. It is not a pleasant experience, whatever the
outcome, to stand in the dock at the Old Bailey. Up there
you feel very much an exhibit. Below are the lawyers, as
busy as ever; counsel for the two sides engaged in their
habitual confidential jokes. One will win, one will lose; in
any event they will be all right. There are the ushers, the
real masters of the court. They have the speculating over-
confidence of comfortable men in their comfortable place

of work. They seize every chance to be obsequious to the judge or counsel and every chance to be insolent to the public or the accused.

There were two details which particularly struck me. The first was the private grandstand near the judge's 'throne' to which his friends could be admitted, at his invitation, to watch him at work. 'Black cap day', when death sentences were passed, was always a popular occasion. The other was a detail visible only from inside the dock itself. When you enter it for your trial you mount the steps from the well of the court and a prison warder locks the door until you are acquitted. Although the proceedings in our case were only a formality, there was a uniformed warder on duty in the dock, and out of habit he locked the door behind us. He had to unlock it to let us out. As I passed him I glanced at his face. He did not seem to share my elation. But the detail which I will never forget, the detail which is visible only from inside the dock, is of the other flight of stairs leading out of that place, the stairs you take down to the cells. No. 1 Court is a massively panelled place. There are the carved coat of arms, the red-leather benches, the gleaming brass railings. And everywhere else there is oak panelling. It has an atmosphere of learning as well as discipline. But below eye-level, on the stairs down to the cells, the wood panelling is replaced by white tiles. The walls are tiled; the steps are stone. There, at a glance, was the horror of confinement and despair. That is the world to which prisoners descend. No one tiles walls unless they are to be washed frequently.

Criminal defamatory libel, the means chosen by this enraged millionaire to improve the standard of the British Press, was one of the offences which emerged from the sixteenth-century jurisdiction of the Court of Star Chamber. It is a remarkable old law, well adapted for its original purpose of arbitrary repression and well suited to the world of honour, privilege and action. According to the report of the Faulks Committee on Defamation (1975), its origins

> appear to lie in the spoken word. King Alfred, for example, is said to have decreed that a slanderer should lose his tongue or (at the miscreant's option) his head, but the slanderers whom they wanted to discourage in early times were those who spread rumours against the government. The Statute of Westminster the First (1275) made it an offence to spread rumours against the government unless and until the person accused produced into court the first author of the rumour.
>
> But the individual's reputation was important too, on the assumption that the liberty of the subject is imperfect unless his character is protected. According to Holt the laws of England took very early notice of slander, both as an injury to the individual and as an offence against the public peace. 'Libel,' he says, 'was only scarcely mentioned in an unlettered age.' In the thirteenth century the local English courts dealt with slander as both a crime and a tort.

The Court of Star Chamber was at one time concerned to discourage duelling. It wanted those who felt their honour had been impugned to take to the law instead, and so it declared itself ready to punish defamatory libels whose publication might have led to a breach of the peace. This crime has always borne a resemblance to the duels which it replaced. When the Star Chamber was abolished in 1641 its jurisdiction passed to the Court of King's Bench, which continued to develop the crime of defamatory libel.

> The reason for libel being a crime was because it might tend towards a breach of the peace. For example: 'Libel is ranked among criminal offences because of its supposed tendency to arouse angry passion, provoke revenge and thus endanger the public peace (1878).' 'Hawkins puts the

whole criminality of libels on private persons, as
distinguished from the civil liability of those who publish
them, on their tendency to disturb the public peace (1884)',
and 'An indictment for libel is only justified when it affects
the public as an attempt to disturb the public peace' (Lord
Coleridge in 1888).

From the start, criminal libel involved unpleasant
punishments. The removal of the tongue, favoured by
King Alfred, was replaced by whipping, branding and
mutilation; the ears of the convicted man could be cut off or
his nose slit. Where the defamatory matter concerned the
government, prosecutions were directed by the Attorney-
General in person. Normal committal proceedings could
thus be avoided, and packed juries, known as 'special'
juries, were allowed. Criminal libel was frequently the
weapon chosen by the government as a means to silence its
critics. Distinguished victims in the seventeenth and
eighteenth centuries included Daniel Defoe and Tobias
Smollett. John Wilkes was prosecuted for his criticism of
Lord Bute. It 'criminalized', as one might say now, William
Cobbett for his denunciation of policy in Ireland, Leigh
Hunt for exposing the savage floggings administered in the
Army and other writers for questioning the sanity of
George IV and for drawing attention to the Peterloo
Massacre. In short, it is a criminal offence with a
thoroughly disreputable history, and it has been con-
sistently used by those in power to punish citizens who
have sought to expose the abuse of power.

Its record in the non-political category is hardly more
impressive. In 1879 a journalist who wrote that Lillie
Langtry was having an affair with the Prince of Wales
(which she was) was imprisoned for criminal libel. The
editor of the *North London Press* who accurately exposed a
scandal centring on a homosexual brothel in Cleveland
Street was imprisoned in 1890. Cecil Chesterton was fined

for criminal libel in 1913 for writing about the Marconi affair. Even Cardinal Newman, in his younger days, was convicted of the offence after denouncing a defrocked priest as a liar and lecher. The priest was both, but the jury, in a fit of anti-clerical enthusiasm, ignored all the evidence and convicted Newman anyway. Dr Newman was not the last person to suffer from the unpredictable character of an English libel jury.

The most remarkable statements have become the grounds for a criminal libel charge: that the Duke of Brunswick was 'someone few people would care to have in their house' (1850), that a French count was 'selling the corpses of dead French soldiers back to the French Army as edible meat' (1884) and that Napoleon was a 'tyrant worthy to be deposed' (1803). The last case was brought by Addington's government after the Peace of Amiens. The case had to be dropped between conviction and sentence due to the government's renewed attempts to depose the tyrant in question.

Reading about those caught up in such cases is like a bad dream of the pre-democracy, of Tudor intrigue or of the Crimean age. It would be no surprise if this law had been confined to the history books. The extraordinary thing about the criminal libel law is that it is current; indeed, as recently as 1936 it was extended. It must also be one of the most difficult charges on the statute book to defend oneself against. No one pays damages in England for publishing a fact which is proved to be true. But you can go to prison for it. It is no defence to a charge of criminal libel that what you have published is true, unless its publication is also held to be for the public benefit. In other words, in English law you can be imprisoned by the state for publishing truthful statements which you cannot be made to pay damages for.

It is one of the basic tenets of criminal law that a guilty

intention must have been formed as well as a guilty act committed – but not in criminal libel. You may have an honest belief in the truth of what you publish, yet that is no defence. You may not even know that publication has taken place. If the court decides that you *should have known* about it – as, for instance, in the case of an editor who falls asleep after lunch instead of reading an article submitted (as happens now and again) – his negligent lack of knowledge would be no defence.

It is an even more fundamental principle of criminal law that an accused person is innocent until proved guilty – but not in criminal libel. It is not for the prosecutor in criminal libel to prove that a statement is untrue. It is for the defendant to establish his innocence by proving the truth of the statement. You are guilty until you can prove yourself innocent. Where a man is prosecuted for publishing a criminal libel, and where he did publish the statement and it was not an occasion of privilege (as in a court or parliamentary report), he has only one defence: that the statement was true *and* that its publication was for the public benefit. But in the case of *Goldsmith* v. *Pressdram* even that defence was not available. The reason was that Goldsmith had already started an action in civil libel and *Private Eye*, in attempting to settle the action, had apologized and agreed that the statement could not be justified. In other words, Goldsmith or, to be more exact, his legal advisers had exploited a situation in which they were entitled to start a civil action, to reach a point in negotiations where the defence of justification had been excluded, then to switch to a criminal prosecution in which no other defence was available.

Perhaps because it is such a disgraceful law,* criminal libel had fallen into relative disuse during this century, particularly with regard to actions against newspapers.

* 'A monstrous offence': J. R. Spencer, *Criminal Law Review* (1977).

Before the Goldsmith case the last prosecution in respect
of a criminal libel in a newspaper had been that of Lord
Alfred Douglas by Winston Churchill in 1923. Douglas,
who seems to have only really come alive in a libel court
(Oscar Wilde had been imprisoned after unsuccessfully
prosecuting his father for libel, and Douglas was himself
prosecuted for libel three times), was on this occasion
prosecuted after printing in his newspaper *Plain English*
that Churchill had conspired with a financier to falsify
reports of the Battle of Jutland (Churchill was First Lord
of the Admiralty at the time), so that he could make a
killing on the Stock Exchange. Lord Alfred Douglas was
found guilty and served six months in prison, so following
briefly in his distinguished mentor's footsteps.

One of Douglas's previous prosecutions had been by
Robert Ross, Wilde's friend and literary executor, who
objected to Douglas's calling him a homosexual. Ross lost
the case, thus ensuring that both Douglas and he repeated
history even more exactly, but Ross, unlike Wilde, was not
jailed for his proclivities; society by then had presumably
grown tired of intervening in these screaming matches. It
completes the pattern neatly to add that on the third
occasion when Douglas was prosecuted, successfully this
time, it was by his own father-in-law. There must have
been something in the Douglas nursery air. They should
have tethered a cow outside the windows to sweeten the
atmosphere with her breath.

After the case of *Churchill* v. *Douglas* the lawyers
slumbered. It was widely held, and invariably laid down in
the textbooks, that it was not possible to bring a criminal
libel action against a newspaper unless the publication of
the item was likely to have resulted in a breach of the
peace. In fact, one appeal case in 1936 held that this was
not a necessary ingredient of the offence. This case (R. v.
Wicks) was half-forgotten until the Faulks Committee's

report drew attention to it. Even then the matter passed without general comment until Goldsmith's legal advisers, possibly encouraged by the report, brought a prosecution against *Private Eye*. They had by that time issued three civil writs, but there was nothing preventing them from both gaining damages in civil law and bringing a criminal case for the same libel.

Leave to bring the criminal case had been given in April 1976. The case was set down for prosecution in May of the following year, by which time public interest in the outcome was considerable. Important issues of law and justice had been raised. The case had been followed with the closest attention in the financial world, where Goldsmith was regarded as a controversial figure anyway, and this interest was even keener because Jim Slater, the former chairman of Slater Walker, the public company which Goldsmith had been appointed to run by the Bank of England, was facing an extradition application by the Singapore government to stand trial for fraud. The criminal libel case had also been closely followed by Members of Parliament – at Westminster the magazine had many enemies and some friends. Jeremy Thorpe, the former leader of the Liberal Party, had, after his sudden retirement, followed Goldsmith's lead in threatening to bring a criminal action against *Private Eye*. Furthermore, the magazine's readers had subscribed £40,000 towards an appeal fund, and the list of subscribers included some surprising figures. (One signed himself 'an impoverished member of the House of Lords and a member of Her Majesty's Privy Council and a Queen's Counsel who prefers open justice to money'.) In short, the case was regarded, both within and outside the legal profession, as 'historic'. And it was, of course, of vital concern to the Press. At this point the London *Evening Standard* came on the market. Goldsmith decided to accept an apology and payment of his costs, and agreed damages of £45,000.

There were certain serious theoretical drawbacks to the settlement which was then reached. First, the new state of the law was most unsatisfactory. The freedom of the Press had been substantially narrowed, and there had not even been a trial, let alone an appeal (which both sides had stated they would take as far as they could).

Second, this was not a civil action brought purely to redress a shattered reputation. The public interest was supposedly committed to a trial. The libel was purportedly so serious that the magazine could face an unlimited fine and its editor and reporter could face up to three years' imprisonment each.

Third, as a prosecution it involved public money and judicial time. Such a case, if brought by a public prosecutor, would be dropped only if it collapsed (if the accused or a vital witness died, for example, or if essential evidence were destroyed). This was not the case here. In fact, the essential prosecution case had been heard by a judge in the preliminary application one year earlier.

Of these the element of public interest was the most puzzling. As a private prosecutor Goldsmith was in the position of a citizen who has apprehended someone in the act of committing a criminal offence (an offence 'against the Peace of our Sovereign Lady the Queen') and is public-spirited enough to bring a case about it. He was exercising a right which existed before the Norman Conquest. It has been reduced to the extent that, for criminal libel, that right is denied to citizens except in cases of exceptional seriousness where the public interest is exceptionally heavily involved. The normal sequel in the case of other serious crimes is that when a prosecution has been started privately the case is taken over by the Public Prosecutor, examined in the public interest and either dropped or prosecuted. In this case the Attorney-General discussed this possibility with the Director of Public Prosecutions and then issued a statement saying that they had agreed that 'the public interest did not require them to intervene'. So, from the point of view of any privately arranged settlement, the element of public interest should have been fatal. In the public interest the prosecution had to be brought; Mr Justice Wien had said so. In the public interest it had to be brought privately; the Attorney-General had said so. How, then, could it be dropped after confidential negotiations between the parties, merely as a matter of their mutual private advantage, just as though this were a civil libel suit? Without the elusive element of public interest, it began to look as though criminal libel were just a means of adding a prison sentence to the pitfalls which awaited those who attempted to exercise freedom of publication. This was not a remedy that was generally available, of course. The man wishing to wield this stick had to have special resources – the ability to make a big noise before a High Court judge about 'exceptionally serious allegations', the importance of himself, the public interest. But when the matter could be settled in such a way, without the public interest being consulted, was he not revealed as just another litigant seeking to defend his reputation and accepting instead damages, an apology, a correction and a contribution to his costs? The settlement was, oddly enough, as unsatisfactory as the original decision to allow the prosecution.

In the words of Lord Shawcross, Q C, who wrote a long article on the subject in *The Times* under the headline 'We must not allow criminal laws to be used in private vendettas':

> It is an odd circumstance that the indictment did not follow the customary precedent of including some such words as 'contrary to the Peace of our Sovereign Lady the Queen' and this omission might well have formed a reason for a

motion to quash the indictment had the prosecution not
been withdrawn. At least the draughtsman did not
substitute 'contrary to the peace of our Sir James
Goldsmith'. Yet that is exactly what this case was about.

At the time leave to prosecute had been given, Mr
Goldsmith had received a full apology, which could have
been widely published: there were many civil actions
pending for libel damages in which (although Lord
Denning in a minority judgment had pronounced some of
them an abuse of legal process) substantial damages might
have been awarded. But Mr Goldsmith wished, not
unnaturally, to vindicate his character by securing the
criminal conviction of his false detractors. And so he went
to war against them. Now developing an interest himself
in the Press, but with his reputation in the City said by *The
Times* financial editor 'to be poor' (May 17), he
understandably wishes to be seen with (*pace* Mr Dubček) a
more human face, and so he made what Mr Justice Bristow
is said to have described as a 'treaty of peace'.

The criminal law, however, should not be used as a
weapon in personal vendettas between private individuals.
Once started, an official prosecution proceeds in the name
of the Crown, costs being payable out of public funds and
its course depending only on the public interest.

Then, referring to the settlement, he wrote:

It is certainly difficult to suppose in the light of his
expressed reasoning that he [Mr Justice Wien] would have
granted leave to prosecute if he had thought that the
prosecution might be 'settled' at the whim of the private
prosecutor as part of a package deal or 'treaty of peace'
between the parties. Yet so it was.

Two weeks ago, in what had all the appearance of inspired
and orchestrated press publicity, it was said that the whole
matter had been settled: it had been agreed that not only the
civil proceedings but also the criminal prosecution would be
withdrawn. It would be 'dropped'. Not a word about the

Crown nor about the need to secure the consent of the court. And the consideration was stated to be the publication of an apology (before and anticipating the court's consent) in the evening paper favoured by Sir James, and the payment over a period of £30,000. It was a package deal. But it improperly prejudged the decision of the court. I have no doubt that the lawyers on both sides were no party to this.

Lord Shawcross added:

> But Mr Justice Bristow had to consider whether it was in the public interest to allow to be withdrawn a prosecution which 'it was perfectly right to start' in the public interest. Nobody doubts that it was in the interest of Sir James Goldsmith to withdraw. But there is no judicial presumption that the public interest necessarily and always coincides with the interest of Sir James.

Goldsmith has since said that one reason why he settled the case was that, following all the publicity it had received, *Private Eye* might have either been acquitted or received a minimal fine. That seems to put his true position very clearly. A man who believes he has apprehended a criminal does not drop the prosecution because he thinks that the suspect will be acquitted. He prosecutes more vigorously. Nor does the 'good citizen' drop a prosecution because the likely penalty will be too light. It is only in the Soviet Union that prosecutors decide penalties. The fact is that Goldsmith was never truly a 'prosecutor'. He was simply an aggrieved plaintiff who had discovered that he might be able to dish out a criminal conviction as well as recover damages in the normal way.

But at least his fears about victory were shared by *Private Eye*. Both sides evidently regarded the outcome with some trepidation, a tribute to the caution of their legal advisers. Both James Comyn and Lewis Hawser had spent many fruitless hours trying to arrange a settlement. Mr Comyn had gone so far as to warn his clients to turn up at the Old Bailey with toothbrushes, on the grounds that the trial judge might easily withdraw bail for the length of the trial. This slightly chilling advice was probably intended more as a warning to clear the mind than as practical help. Judging by reports of washing facilities in London's remand prisons, toothbrushes would have been of little use.

As for the defence of the action, it would, in the understated opinion of Desmond Browne, Mr Comyn's junior counsel, have raised 'difficult questions of law'. 'In particular,' argued Mr Browne, 'counsel will have to argue that the case of R. v. *Wicks* is distinguishable and/or wrongly decided . . . The points of law as to what libels are as grave as to merit a criminal prosecution and whether the prosecution have to show a real likelihood of a breach of the peace will almost certainly go to the Lords.'

There certainly seemed to be ample grounds for questioning the *Wicks* decision, though in the absence of a courtroom the debate had to be mounted in the pages of *The Times*. Peter Carter-Ruck, a leading libel solicitor and a veteran adversary of *Private Eye*, made the point that 'Since no libel published in a newspaper is either likely to cause a breach of the peace or leave a complainant without a remedy in a civil action for damages, it can only be in very exceptional circumstances that anyone should seek leave to proceed against a newspaper by way of criminal prosecution.' He added that *Private Eye*, in his experience, always met its legal obligation to pay damages and costs.

Sir Robert McEwen, the editor of *Gatley on Libel and Slander*, pointed out that although the likelihood of a breach of the peace was no longer, following *Wicks*, a necessary ingredient of the offence of criminal libel, its likelihood *was* one of the considerations to be taken into account by the judge who had to decide whether to allow the prosecution to proceed. It was not clear that Mr Justice Wien *had* taken this into account.

Another correspondent, William Kimber, pointed out that before the confusion introduced by *Wicks*, criminal libel had been an instrument for preserving order. Truth was not a defence unless combined with public benefit, and the offence was committed even if the libel was published only to the person defamed. The intention of the law was to punish a provocation to violence. *Wicks*, therefore, had changed the entire basis of the law, not normally an initiative which the Court of Appeal was encouraged to take. Furthermore, it appeared to be in conflict with earlier precedents.

On technical grounds it seems clear that the defence of the case was by no means a lost cause. I myself thought it inconceivable that one could be sent to prison in England for innocently repeating a mistake made in someone else's newspaper article. But the lawyers may have been right; they probably knew a thing or two about miscarriages of justice. One of them, indeed, described all jury trials as 'a lottery at best'.

The only other formality in our trial had been the entry of the panel of jurors who would have judged us. They came in, with a considerable clatter, at the back of the room, ready no doubt for the next case, and I turned to look at the people who might have held my freedom in their hands. It was not an encouraging sight. They were a representative cross-section of youthful Londoners, incurious, slightly intimidated and *bored*. Knowing some of the cheap tricks of advocacy, the numerous permitted means of arranging the evidence in such a way as to produce a misleading effect, all the professional, mountebank skills of the adversary system of trial – which is the pride and joy of our legal system – I suddenly understood what the lawyer meant when he described a jury trial as a lottery. It would be a dreadful thing to be locked up because a jury had become too bored to follow the case. One of them was already so bored that he was blowing bubble-gum, at 9.30 a.m., in the Old Bailey. I think of those jurors whenever I read another instalment of the long-running serial 'Our Legal System is the Best in the World'.

My own belief in the truth of what I had written had been absolute at the time, but would the bubble-gummers have been convinced? We did have some steadfast witnesses, determined, despite a certain amount of discouragement, to come forward and explain how the mistakes in the article came innocently to be made. There were two witnesses who would have reminded the jury of the story's origins: James Fox of the *Sunday Times* and Charles Benson of the *Daily Express*, a friend of both Lucan and Elwes. But there was another journalist, also working for Express Newspapers, whose evidence would have been invaluable but who declined to give evidence lest it damage her career. She could not be subpoenaed by the defence because it would have exposed her as one of *Private Eye*'s sources and so breached the confidentiality every journalist offers to his sources. Her career, I am pleased to say, continues to prosper.

The final, last-minute surprise came in the person of the judge. There are fifteen regular judges at the Old Bailey but our case had been given to none of them. Instead Mr Justice Bristow had been specially summoned from the High Court. Bristow J. was, I believe, at that time the only living judge to have taken a criminal libel trial against a publication. It had been for an 'obscene' libel and the defendant had been found guilty. Mr Justice Bristow's appearance on the bench, if the case had gone ahead, would have seemed ominous. An academic inquiry into that intriguing black hole of the legal administraton, how judges are selected at the Old Bailey, would seem to be long overdue.

There is something contagious about criminal laws resurrected from near-burial. Just as Oscar Wilde's prosecution of the Marquess of Queensberry led to a flurry of criminal libel actions, so did Sir James Goldsmith's. First the leader of the Liberal Party, Jeremy Thorpe, MP, anxious to avoid a prosecution for conspiracy to murder, threatened *Private Eye* again. Then Brian Sedgemore, MP, urged his party's Attorney-General to prosecute the editor of the *Daily Mail* for libel after the latter had unwittingly published a forged letter which suggested official corruption.

Then a rogue called Roger Gleaves, a convicted pederast, actually prosecuted the authors of a book which exposed his activities. Mr Gleaves too would seem to have got his inspiration from Sir James Goldsmith. His case, in 1979, led to further calls for reform of the law, this time by five judges of the House of Lords. The Gleaves trial provided an interesting echo of the Goldsmith case. The trial judge was Mr Justice Comyn, who as James Comyn, QC, had led for the defence of *Private Eye*. In his summing up he too called for the reform of the law and said that it was wholly unfitted to modern times. 'I am one of the many judges,' he said, 'who consider the law of criminal libel and of private prosecutions as extremely unsatisfactory.' The jury took one hour to acquit the authors, John Willis and Michael Deakin. Following the acquittal, counsel for the defence, Mr Richard Rampton, said: 'This prosecution has been a complete disgrace. It should never have been brought and the law of criminal libel should have been left in disuse.' This was a refreshing development in Mr Rampton's thinking. He had been the energetic junior counsel for the *prosecution* in the Goldsmith case. Nothing, of course, has since been done to reform the law of criminal libel.

But the revival of the law of criminal libel against newspapers was not Sir James's only attempt to reform newspaper law. His name has also entered the standard works of reference as plaintiff in the case of *Goldsmith* v. *Sperrings Ltd*, a case which started before a High Court master and ended before the Appeals Committee of the House of Lords with victory for Goldsmith and a ludicrous ruling from the Court of Appeal that a plaintiff in libel could sue any of the distributors of the offending material, whether it be a newsboy or even a man who handed a newspaper to his neighbour on the bus.

This case started when Goldsmith, having started civil proceedings against *Private Eye*, issued eighty additional writs against forty newsagents and local newspaper distributors in respect of two of the three civil libel actions. The normal practice was to proceed against the principal publishers of an alleged libel and to take action against newspaper distributors only as a last resort if the principals were unable to meet awarded damages. When issuing these writs, Goldsmith offered to withdraw them if the particular newsagent would agree *never* to distribute the magazine again. As a result, *Private Eye* lost 12,000 copies, about one-eighth of its circulation. But seventeen distributors applied to have the writs against them struck out as being 'frivolous, vexatious and an abuse of the process of the courts', since they were intended not to recover damages but to interfere with the magazine's circulation. This application was successful. Goldsmith appealed to the High Court and won. The seventeen distributors appealed to the Court of Appeal.

The decision of those seventeen individual news retailers to oppose the Goldsmith juggernaut was in an heroic tradition. None of them made sufficient money from selling *Private Eye* to justify the battle, which they seem to have entered in the spirit of bloody-minded independence. But there is a long history of independence in the newspaper-distribution trade, even though it is today dominated by the near-monopolists. As long ago as 1831, when the Whig government tried to suppress a radical paper, the *Poor Man's Guardian*, by taxing every copy with a 4d. stamp it was the newsagents and street hawkers who kept the paper on the streets after its editor had been sentenced to six months' imprisonment. The distributors, like the editor, were jailed week after week but did not let up until the editor had won his freedom.

A similar victory was not to be repeated on this occasion. The Court of Appeal decided, by two to one, that Goldsmith was entitled to sue the distributors before his other remedies against *Private Eye* were exhausted, and also held that in offering to withdraw the writs against those of the distributors who undertook *never* to sell the magazine again, Goldsmith was merely trying to protect his reputation; he was not trying to suppress the magazine. Lord Denning, the Master of the Rolls, dissented from the majority in a memorably blunt judgment. Lord Denning said that if these writs against newsagents were justified, it was grounds for suing anyone who handed a copy of the magazine to his neighbour. The only previous cases in which secondary distributors had been sued for libel had been when they had, for some reason, known of the libellous contents before undertaking distribution. To shut off the channels of distribution was a collateral purpose outside the proper scope of the legal process. And if distribution channels were blocked so that a ban was placed on the distribution of even one periodical, that was intrusion into the freedom of the Press.

The majority judgments were based on a different interpretation of the facts and on the belief that in suing numerous individual newspaper sellers Goldsmith was merely trying to vindicate his reputation. The court ruled that it was perfectly permissible to join any 'distributor' to the action. And the fact that a mere threat of litigation had been enough to persuade many distributors never to handle the magazine again was not enough to persuade it to intervene. If, by so doing, Goldsmith was threatening a paper's existence, then he was merely exercising his legal right, and that was a matter for Parliament, not the courts.

This ruling represented a substantial increase in the room for manoeuvre allowed to a plaintiff in libel. Leave to appeal to the House of Lords was refused – despite the fact that the House of Lords had never considered the question of the liability in libel of newspaper distributors. Auberon Waugh commented on the Court of Appeal's decision in a somewhat intemperate article in the *Spectator* of 5 March 1977:

> Lord Denning's decision, which, although overruled by his two colleagues, will surely echo down the corridors of history as a reminder that not all Englishmen at the present time are imbecile, illiterate or senile, dealt not only with the particular absurdity with which the law was confronted – 'no private individual should be allowed to stifle a publication on his own estimate of its worthlessness' – but also demolished the legal myth that distributors are liable in law for any libel in the material they handle. Such a superstition, reveals his Lordship, has no backing in case or statute law . . .
>
> Unfortunately, such blinding common sense did not appeal to his Lordship's two colleagues. The less said about their judgments the better, but perhaps two quotations will serve to illuminate the depths of their incomprehension:
>
> Lord Justice Bridge: 'If *Private Eye* was engaged in the courageous exposure of public evils, no action taken by Sir James would impede that righteous crusade.'
>
> Lord Justice Scarman: 'Finally, the decision on the

present appeal was not helped by reference to Sir James's wealth. Wealth might well have afforded him the chance of invoking the law to protect his reputation in a way in which, alas, a poorer man could not.'

Oh, alas, alas, *toi-même*, ducky. If the poor, as well as the grotesquely rich, could stifle distribution in this way, not a single newspaper, magazine or comic cut would ever be published.

Although the 'distributors' case' was a handsome victory for Goldsmith, and ample vindication of his aggressive tactics, it did very little to endear him to the newspaper proprietors and journalists of England, among whom he had a sincere desire to number himself.

Goldsmith's growing fascination with the Press as a whole became clearer as his battle with *Private Eye* progressed. He wrote an open letter to the Press Council alleging that reports in two national newspapers about the series of cases were written by journalists who had connections with *Private Eye*. He then threw some light on his own philosophy of Press freedom. Presumably, he said, when newspapers wrote about a legal action they usually did so as independent commentators. While the action was before the courts, editors did not knowingly open their columns to one of the litigants so that only one side of the case was publicized. If they were to do so, no doubt they would consider it fair to disclose the fact. Goldsmith suggested that editors should maintain a register disclosing the private interests of journalists. He said that partiality of reporters was one of the fundamental issues that would emerge during the course of his legal actions, and he trusted that it would be examined later by the government's Royal Commission on the Press. Then, possibly dissatisfied by the lack of response to this Jeffersonian treatise, Goldsmith began to consider acquiring a newspaper of his own. He bought into Express Newspapers (which owned the *Evening*

Standard) through his food company, Cavenham. Then he bought a 45 per cent share in the French weekly *L'Express* through his French holding company. At the same time he was frustrated in his attempt to buy the London Sunday paper the *Observer* and was also reported to be an unsuccessful bidder in the United States for *Esquire* and *New York Magazine*.

Then in April 1977, one month before the date of the trial, the London *Evening Standard* came on the market and it looked as though this would be purchased by its only rival, the London *Evening News*. At that time Goldsmith held 35 per cent of the non-voting shares in Express Newspapers, which owned the *Standard*, and he was invited by the board to intervene. He expressed a formal interest, thereby blocking the rival bid, and during the weeks that followed the board of Express Newspapers strongly advised him to drop his prosecution of *Private Eye*. For Goldsmith it must have seemed like a return to the real world, the world of takeovers and press releases, of telegrams and anger, of horse-trading and share movements – the world of serious leapfrog. The mediator on Express Newspapers' side was Simon Jenkins, then editor of the *Standard*. He denied that settlement of the criminal libel case was a condition of Goldsmith's bid for the *Evening Standard* but said that it represented a 'real problem', that the *Standard*'s staff were extremely worried that the case was continuing and that it was seen as a 'festering sore' between Goldsmith and Fleet Street. So, with his eyes set firmly on a newspaper of his own, Goldsmith decided to drop the case. By then Lady Annabel Birley and Lady Falkender had presumably been avenged somewhere on the way.

As a matter of fact, not all Fleet Street did consider that Goldsmith was a 'real problem'. When he eventually launched his own news magazine he had no difficulty in recruiting staff. Even his bid for the *Standard* was welcomed by the *Daily Telegraph*. The 'diversity of the Press' was at risk; the 'jobs of men' who had spent a lifetime working for the Press monopolists were insecure. 'From this possibility,' prayed the leader writer of the *Daily Telegraph*, 'may Sir James deliver us.' The article recalled Chesterton's poem 'When I Came Back to Fleet Street', in which he set forth a fantasy about returning to liberate the prisoners who toiled there, only to find that they had served too long. They were 'chained to the rich by ruin'; they could only peer up at his banners and shrink from the prospect of escape, preferring what they knew – 'All the truth they talk in hell,/And all the lies they write'.

Leaving the Old Bailey, I had a sense of quitting a murky world in which we had all, for the past eighteen months, been stumbling around in the dark. In the street outside the Central Criminal Court it was a sunny day. With a spring in the step and lightened hearts, Ingrams and I went our separate ways.

Lord Cardigan cracked his horsewhip at the *Morning Chronicle*'s leader writer in 1839; Sir James Goldsmith 'manhandled' a photographer from the *Daily Express* in 1978. Lord Lucan was removed from the bench in 1842; John Addey was removed from the bench in 1978. Both Cardigan and Goldsmith brought private prosecutions for criminal libel. Lord Cardigan escaped any serious prosecution for attempted murder in 1841; Lord Lucan was never brought before a court for attempted murder in 1974. The nobility of the early nineteenth century considered themselves to be above the law; some members of the Clermont Club, 130 years later, considered themselves outside it.

No doubt it was all coincidence, but at least these events formed a sort of pattern, one which made more sense than the trail of havoc that we had been following. Lord Lucan, who wanted to recover his children and who succeeded in arranging matters so that he could never see them again; Goldsmith, who wanted to own a newspaper that would expose the Soviet conspiracy against the Western media and who succeeded in silencing the one magazine that might have investigated MI5's evidence of Soviet conspiracies. And then there were the victims: Sandra Rivett and Dominick Elwes dead; Veronica Lucan's life a ruin, as was Leslie Paisner's; John Addey disgraced. And there were still a couple of clinks left in the phantom's chain.

Although Goldsmith dropped the criminal libel prosecution, he never did buy the *Evening Standard*. In June another prospective purchaser appeared and Goldsmith failed to match the bid. When Express Newspapers was sold it was the end of the Aitken family's connection with Fleet Street. Laura Aitken has since said that it was she who persuaded her father not to sell the paper to Goldsmith. She had once been a close friend of Dominick Elwes.

'A Man not to be Believed in any Particular'

Once the criminal libel case was settled it seemed that both sides could let the matter drop. The ghost of Lord Lucan might finally be laid to rest. One by one, the issues had been overtaken by events. *Private Eye* no longer believed that Goldsmith had attended the lunch party at which ways of helping the fugitive were discussed. Goldsmith no longer thought that *Private Eye* was accusing him of being a member of a criminal conspiracy. No allegations against Mr Levine were being pursued, and the men who had made the original allegations had long since withdrawn them. Goldsmith was no longer claiming a right of veto over what appeared in *Private Eye*, and he was no longer under the impression that *Private Eye* was attacking him as part of its communist ambitions to destroy the City of London. Sir James busied himself with his plans to launch *Now!* magazine, the publication which would give him the platform he had so long desired.

Legally there were only two minor loose ends to be tidied up. During the battle with *Private Eye*, Goldsmith

had named a *Sunday Times* journalist, Philip Knightley, as a
'collaborator' of *Private Eye* in a letter to Lord Shawcross,
then chairman of the Press Council. Mr Knightley issued a
writ for libel in July 1976, in the heat of the day. This
action was settled in 1978, when Goldsmith apologized,
withdrew and paid damages to Mr Knightley. Later in the
year Michael Gillard accepted an apology and substantial
damages from his former friend, John Addey, in settlement
of the allegation of blackmail that Mr Addey had made in
his affidavit. *The Times* reported that:

> Mr John Previte, for Mr Gillard, told Mr Justice O'Connor
> that from time to time Mr Gillard had provided
> information to the satirical magazine, *Private Eye*, and had
> been a defendant in actions brought by Sir James
> Goldsmith arising out of publications in that magazine.
> Mr Gillard had been on friendly terms with Mr Addey
> for several years, during which time he had proved a
> helpful and reliable informant. Mr Gillard knew him to be
> not unsympathetic also to *Private Eye*, counsel added. He
> therefore sought Mr Addey's help in pursuing certain
> inquiries in connection with that litigation.
> In conversation and in an affidavit Mr Addey alleged
> that Mr Gillard had been applying improper pressure on
> him to secure the information that he sought.
> 'It was suggested that Mr Gillard had threatened Mr
> Addey that if he did not assist in the investigation *Private
> Eye* would publish damaging material about Mr Addey and
> his firm and it was alleged that Mr Gillard had been guilty
> of blackmailing Mr Addey,' Mr Previte said. 'Mr Addey
> accepts that Mr Gillard did not make any threats
> whatsoever and was never in any sense guilty of
> blackmailing him.'

That should have been the end of the matter, except for
another initiative taken by Sir James Goldsmith. The
settlement with *Private Eye* was formalized on 16 May

1977. Four days later Goldsmith, who knew, of course, that Gillard was suing Addey for libel, chose to write a letter to William Deedes, editor of the *Daily Telegraph*, in which he repeated Addey's allegations. Formerly he had repeated these only orally, so limiting any litigation to an action for slander. By writing the allegations in a letter Goldsmith opened himself to a libel action, which duly commenced.

If Goldsmith's use of the criminal libel law had left the criminal courts in a state of some confusion and caused general damage in pursuit of a particular end which he eventually abandoned, his decision to defend himself against Michael Gillard's libel action went further, finally leaving even the Court of Appeal helpless and unable to right a wrong. Once again, Goldsmith's use of the law depended heavily on his personal intervention. The hearing that followed his decision to defend Gillard's libel action was a remarkable miscarriage of justice.

There are two rules of evidence which should be remembered when considering this case. The first is that in a libel action it is not up to the plaintiff to prove his good character. Michael Gillard did not have to prove that he was *not* a blackmailer. Goldsmith had to prove that he was. As defendant he had to justify the serious allegations he had made. Journalists, faced with a libel action, have complained bitterly about this position for years. Now, it seemed, one of them was to benefit from it. The only way to prove an allegation in an English court is by evidence, the testimony of witnesses, or documents, or other relevant matters or objects. Goldsmith produced only the affidavits sworn by Leslie Paisner and signed by John Addey. He called no witnesses. Addey himself, whose office was about a mile away from the High Court and who was the only witness to the alleged blackmail, never appeared in court.

The second rule of evidence to remember is that 'hearsay evidence' is generally not admitted. A witness cannot repeat as a fact something which he has merely heard from someone else. That is hearsay. If a statement is to be put before the jury as a fact, the original speaker must give evidence. Nevertheless, Goldsmith was allowed to give hearsay evidence. When he was asked to explain why he believed Addey had been blackmailed, despite the fact that Addey had since denied it, Goldsmith was allowed to answer, 'Addey told me . . .,' and so on. At that point the judge, Mr Justice Neill, should have said that the court would hear Addey's explanation only if it were given in person. But he did not do that and Goldsmith continued to say that Addey had withdrawn the allegation only because he did not have enough money to defend Gillard's libel action. That too was hearsay. Since Addey was the owner of a large and successful PR consultancy, and Gillard was a self-employed journalist, this explanation was intrinsically unlikely – but no comment was made about that either. The trial judge allowed the hearsay description of Addey as a 'poor man' to be put to the jury.

Handed this advantage, Sir James went ahead and won the case (in which I was a witness for Michael Gillard). He spent a day and a half in the witness box, putting up another virtuoso performance and delighting some members of the jury. His counsel this time was not the bombastic Lewis Hawser, QC, but the silver-tongued charmer Lord Rawlinson, QC, a softly spoken and insinuating advocate who made the most of the little he had to go on. Nor was Gillard, alas, represented by James Comyn, QC. He had to pay his own costs – *Private Eye*, in a striking act of disloyalty, having refused to back his case – and his pocket did not run to leading counsel.

There was no doubt at all that, even at this extreme, we were still in the world of Lord Lucan. Those present in court included several of his friends. John Aspinall was among them, together with his mother, Lady Osborne. During one lunch adjournment Aspinall was invited to share a taxi by several journalists and was happy to accept until Goldsmith appeared at his elbow and started to abuse the company. Aspinall, looking rather embarrassed, then declined the taxi.

After the jury's verdict Gillard appealed. The comments made by the judges of the Court of Appeal considering his case were to be his only consolation.

The difficulty with Goldsmith's case, according to Lord Justice Templeman, was how to 'get *Hamlet* off the ground without the Prince of Denmark' (i.e. Addey). The only evidence Goldsmith had for the blackmail was Addey's word, later dignified as an unsworn affidavit, later still withdrawn as completely false and, finally, re-alleged. Addey, said Lord Denning, was therefore a man in whom no credence could be placed. The court could understand why he had not been called as a witness. 'No one,' said Lord Denning, 'would believe a word he said.' 'He was not to be believed in any particular,' said Lord Justice Templeman. 'If the jury had believed his affidavit, they were completely wrong.' '[Addey] told so many lies about so many things,' said Lord Denning, '. . . and yet Sir James Goldsmith accepted his affidavit as the gospel truth.'

Concerning the note that Addey put forward as the instrument of blackmail Lord Denning said, 'This document does not look like a blackmailer's note . . . A lot of people have read more into it than I would.' And, concerning the affidavit sworn by the late Leslie Paisner, Lord Denning said that it was a very unnatural form of affidavit from Mr Paisner and almost looked as if it were made under pressure. And of Addey's affidavit Lord Justice Templeman said, 'It's as plain as a pikestaff that there was pressure [on Addey].'

On the question of Addey going back on his accusation because of poverty, as claimed by Goldsmith from the witness box, the court agreed with Gillard's counsel that this claim was not evidence. 'The only *evidence* the jury had heard on the question of Addey's wealth,' said Lord Denning, 'was that he made a lot of money.' It was also true to say that he lived in Albany and had been able to pay £5,000 damages. And yet the trial judge had allowed the suggestion of poverty to be put to the jury as evidence. When Lord Rawlinson, QC, for Sir James Goldsmith, argued that Addey had also been reluctant to defend the action because he did not wish to be exposed as a homosexual, Lord Justice Templeman pointed out that he was *already* exposed as a homosexual, and that the only consequence of retracting his apology to Gillard was to encourage Goldsmith to fight the case in his place, thereby re-exposing his homosexuality all over again.

How, then, did the Court of Appeal come to decide against Gillard? They agreed that the evidence was quite insufficient for a criminal conviction of blackmail, although Goldsmith described his own allegation as 'a grave allegation of a grave crime', and Lord Denning observed that the effect of the jury's decision was the same as if a criminal conviction had taken place. But before 'disturbing' the jury's decision in a civil case the Court had to take the extreme view that *no reasonable jury* could have reached it. And the Court of Appeal instead decided that it was *possible*, however remotely so, that merely as a result of listening to Gillard and Goldsmith a reasonable jury might have decided in the latter's favour. (Although Lord Justice Templeman said, referring to Goldsmith's decisive appearance in the witness box, that it must have added to the jury's confusion 'to have this great financier coming and thundering away for a day and a half'.) None the less, on the possibility, however distant, of a reasonable decision, the appeal was refused.

In view of the negotiations which had earlier taken place between Gillard and Addey, the final result was even more nonsensical. At that time Addey's solicitors, Oswald Hickson, had given an undertaking on behalf of their client that he would never repeat the allegation. During negotiations Addey had never once pleaded the truth of his accusations; the only defence he had considered was privilege, and when that failed he decided to withdraw and settle. Because he was allowed to retract Addey's apology without producing Addey, Goldsmith made a nonsense of the previous settlement in open court. It forced Gillard into a position in which his only redress would have been to sue Addey all over again, but since the case had been settled, that was not possible. And anyway he had no money left. He had even been forced to sell his home. During the case Lord Rawlinson tried to prevent any evidence of Addey's retraction from being put to the jury, but in this at least he failed. Had he succeeded, and so placed the jury even deeper in the dark, it would no doubt have been considered a legitimate tactical victory within the rules of evidence. It would also have been yet another example of how the adversary system of trial obscures the truth rather than revealing it, to the final benefit of no one apart from those who make their living by knowing the rules of evidence.

And so, armed with all the assistance which the legal process had been able to give them, the jury in the case of *Gillard* v. *Goldsmith* retired to cogitate their way towards a 'reasonable' decision. What can be revealed about this mysterious process? Normally nothing, but this case is an exception. For no fewer than three members of the jury in the case of *Gillard* v. *Goldsmith* subsequently expressed doubts about their verdict. A barrister who met one of them by chance, a few days after the case, was told that several of the jurymen had been more anxious to return to their normal life than to consider the evidence. Similar views were expressed to a Fleet Street journalist by one of his neighbours who had served on the jury. And some months later a third member of the jury wrote to the editor of *Private Eye*. He enclosed a donation to Michael Gillard's defence fund and said, 'Our decision has troubled me ever since . . . I hope that Mr Gillard's appeal will be successful.' Under our quaint legal system such direct evidence of a miscarriage of justice could not, of course, be used in the Court of Appeal.

So, with the full approval of the law, Michael Gillard's reputation was impugned by a man who was 'not to be believed in any particular', a self-confessed liar who proved far too slippery ever to give evidence against him in court. In the words of the immortal Beachcomber, 'Justice must not only be done. It must be seen to be believed.'

CONCLUSION

'The Shadow on the Ceiling . . .'

'When it comes to killing,' he went on slowly, 'every man is a specialist . . . The poisoner never strangles, and the strangler does not carry a bludgeon.'

Eric Ambler, *The Intercom Conspiracy*

The bludgeon is silent and comes easily to hand, but it has at least two disadvantages, both of which were evident in the killing of Sandra Rivett. It is liable to make a considerable mess, and it requires a degree of strength. 'A degree' of strength does not mean brute strength. Strong people striking to kill with an unfamiliar implement are liable to underestimate their strength, and the person who killed Sandra Rivett in Lower Belgrave Street certainly did that. She was killed by a blunt instrument, evidently the piece of lead piping which was found in the upstairs cloak-room. At the post-mortem her injuries were listed as four splits in the scalp on the front side of the head, two splits near the neck, heavy bruising on both shoulders and other bruises on the right arm. Death was caused by the scalp wounds and bruising to the brain. So her killer accomplished his work with four blows delivered at the head. He also missed his target about half a dozen times, judging by the injuries to the face, neck and shoulders.

It must be very difficult to use a bludgeon with an effective degree of skill if you cannot get a clear view of your victim. Indeed, there is a party game called 'Are you there, Moriarty?', in which blindfolded opponents who are armed with rolled-up newspapers demonstrate this difficulty. The moral must be: don't try to club anyone to death in the dark. Even using a torch would have its disadvantages. It would leave the attacker with no hand to deal with resistance; the beam would have to be steadily directed on to a moving target; and its wavering light might cause the attacker to misjudge distance. All this might make even a bludgeon quite a tricky weapon to use. A man might give himself a nasty crack over, for example, his own wrist. The problems of using a bludgeon in the dark are easily foreseeable. The police case against Lord Lucan suggested that he had laid a careful plan to do away with his wife, yet the problem of using the bludgeon was apparently one point which escaped his attention.

There is another detail that is inconsistent with the police case: the ferocity of the attack. According to the police account, John Lucan intended to kill his wife by hitting her over the head with a length of lead piping. He then planned to conceal her body in a canvas bag and to dispose of it. A canvas bag has the advantage that it will hold a certain amount of liquid. But it is not waterproof (unlike, for example, a plastic refuse sack). Lucan must have known that if you hit someone over the head hard enough to kill her, she is going to bleed. But if you hit her as hard as you can, six to ten times, there is going to be blood all over the place. A canvas sack will not be able to contain it, and the room will have to be carefully cleaned – when time is at

a premium. For Lucan to have delivered so many unnecessary blows he must have been in a rage or panic.
That state of mind is inconsistent with the condition of
a murderer who is carrying out a cold-blooded plot.
Blind rage and panic are also inconsistent with Lucan's
subsequent behaviour, as described by his wife, in allowing
himself to be talked out of his attack on her, then helping
her upstairs and trying to bandage her wounds. There is
something about the ferocity of the attack on Sandra
Rivett that does not convince one of the presence of John
Lucan.

The police case against Lord Lucan is, of course, a strong
one. It starts with the statement made by Veronica Lucan,
and this was found to be consistent with the forensic
examination that followed. Her statement is partly supported by the evidence of her daughter – then 10 years old
and a highly convincing witness – and it is further supported by forensic examination of the car which Lucan had
borrowed from Michael Stoop and which he was apparently driving on the night in question. Furthermore, the
only brief account Lucan himself gave of events was
contradicted by subsequent investigation.

There is very little doubt that if a murder jury had been
faced with the police evidence presented at Sandra Rivett's
inquest, and with the brief defence Lucan was reported to
have made, they would have found him guilty. But that is
far from saying that he would be found guilty if he were
tried today. Perhaps the police got it right. Or perhaps
they did not. Let us return to Lord Lucan's account of
what happened.

It was his custom to pass the family house in Lower
Belgrave Street on his way back to his own flat near by.
He did this to reassure himself about his children. On the
night of 7 November he happened to be passing at a time
when there was a struggle going on in the basement. He

could see this from the pavement. He thereupon let himself in and interrupted a fight between his wife and an intruder. He slipped in a pool of blood and so was unable to prevent the escape of the unknown assailant. His wife, in her hysterical condition, accused him of hiring the man who had actually killed the nanny in order to kill her. He quietened his wife and started to attend to her wounds, but she ran out of the house. He too left the house because he realized that she would accuse him of the crime. He was indeed covered in blood, and he would be unable to clear himself. It had been 'a night of unbelievable coincidence'. Subsequently the police investigated Lord Lucan's claim that he had seen a struggle from the pavement and decided that it was impossible to see that part of the basement from the pavement. Nor was there any sign of a struggle in that room.

John Lucan's friends, loyal to him after his disappearance, tried to suggest wild alternative scenarios, which tried to implicate just about everyone else who could have been involved. The trouble with advancing ludicrous explanations for the actions of your friends is that the general public is apt to conclude that there can't be a plausible one. However, it is possible to do better than that. It might even be possible to construct a theory of events in Lower Belgrave Street which started with the objective facts and then succeeded in reconciling the statements of both parties. This theory would run as follows.

Sandra Rivett descended to the basement carrying a tray of cups and saucers. Finding the light out of action, she would probably have exclaimed. She would then have continued down the last flight of stairs, presumably heading for a different light switch. She was first attacked at the point where the broken crocks were found. Here she was hit on the head with a length of lead piping. Since there were no signs of a struggle, she can be presumed to have gone down under the first attack, even to have lost consciousness almost immediately. She bled copiously on to the floor, her head amid the broken cups. Her attacker then moved her slightly, perhaps dragging her into a patch of light thrown from the next room, and this left the second pool of blood. He examined her to check whether she was dead. Then he doubled her body up and stuffed it, head and feet first, into a sack. Then, still armed with the lead piping, he mounted the darkened stairs and entered the cloakroom, perhaps thinking of searching the house, perhaps intending to leave by the front door when he was sure the coast was clear.

The second attack, as objectively evidenced, was of a different nature from the first, although the weapon used was the same. It began about twenty minutes after the first attack. It can be distinguished by the fact that blood spilled in it was all of Group A, Lady Lucan's group, while the blood in the basement was of Group B, Sandra Rivett's group. The second attack took place in the hallway and on the stairs leading down to the basement. In the first attack the killer accomplished his purpose with four blows to the skull, but also missed his target at least six times. None the less, when he had finished his victim was dead. In the second attack, against a woman of equivalent size, he landed seven blows to the skull, all between the top of the head and the right forehead. It was a more precise attack, *and yet it did not kill its target.* Indeed, as a result of this attack, Lady Lucan did not even lose consciousness for more than a moment; on the contrary, she was able to fight off her attacker.

It is almost as though these two attacks were made by two different people. But that theory raises its own problems. Could it be that Sandra Rivett was killed on purpose by one man in a frenzy directed against her, and that Veronica Lucan was attacked by a second man, and that it was the second man whom Lucan saw from the pavement? The chain of coincidence in such a case is too long to be worth considering. Furthermore, the police found no evidence of two intruders, nor any sign of forced entry. Then again, Lady Lucan had smears of Group B blood on her clothing, so she must either have come into contact with the man who was covered with Sandra's blood or herself been into the basement. Finally, she had traces of Group B blood under the arch of her shoe. That would suggest that she had trodden in a puddle of such blood, all of which was in the basement. She made no mention, of course, of going into the basement.

The main chance of reconciling the two accounts lies in the possibility that Veronica Lucan, in her shock, confused the man who attacked her in the dark with her husband, who rescued her from that attacker. In the first place she had been struck a severe blow on the head, in the dark, by a silent stranger. 'Later', after a period of struggle, she screamed, and only after that did she recognize her husband's voice telling her to shut up. Following that, her husband did not strike her; instead he thrust his hand down her throat. Could it be that she was unaware that the silent figure in the dark had changed from a man who was trying to kill her into a man who was trying to silence her? It hardly seems likely, yet it would appear to be the only way in which that part of her statement which is supported by forensic evidence can be reconciled with her husband's brief account. But her statement did not end there. It went on, of course, to assert that Lucan had told her that he had 'killed the nanny'. The assertion is irreconcilable with everything he said, but that part of her statement is unsupported by any other evidence and cannot be produced in court for as long as the Lucans remain married. To believe the last part of Lady Lucan's statement you have to believe her word against her husband's, and one jury has already believed her without hesitation. None the less, certain questions are raised and left unanswered by the published accounts of Veronica Lucan's statement.

Why was there Group B blood under the arch of her shoe if she never entered the basement? Why was Group A blood (her group) found on the ceiling of the cloakroom – according to forensic opinion, 'splashed' there by the movements of a bloodstained weapon which was rising and falling – when by her account the struggle took place on the stairs? Why was the bludgeon found in that same cloakroom if it was last used on the stairs? Leaving it in the cloakroom hardly concealed it, and leaving it at all provided dreadful confirmation of her story. How was Veronica Lucan able to survive the attack of a man who had already brutally beaten to death a younger woman of similar size? If the attacker was, as she stated, her husband, how was she able to defeat the attack of such a large man, and how, since they were on terms of cordial hatred, was she able to talk him out of hitting her? Further, to believe the police case, one has to accept that Lord Lucan mistook Mrs Rivett for his wife because it was dark. He failed to recognize the difference in her tread, her outlined shape, the noises she made as she moved, even her probable exclamation when she found the light would not work. After nine years of marriage, that is unlikely.

There is another infelicity in the police account of events, although it does not necessarily work in favour of Lucan's innocence, and that is the question of how the intruder gained entry. The police found no evidence of forced entry and are therefore confident that the murderer entered through the front door. Lucan possessed a Yale key to the front door. The door was normally kept on the chain, but on this occasion it was not chained. If Lucan knew that there was a chain on the front door, why did he assume that he would be able to enter by using his key? If he was planning a murder, he would hardly leave such an important detail to chance. He must have been confident that he could gain entry, so we must conclude he knew that on the nanny's night off the door was always left unchained, so that she could re-enter without disturbing Veronica. The house did, of course, have a back door but the police eliminated the possibility that entry had been gained that way as the yard outside was enclosed by a wall and trellis eighteen feet high. On the evidence that has been presented so far, the police seem to have excluded the possibility of a second intruder rather quickly. It is one thing, and a reasonable thing, to exclude 'intruders' from the inquiry because there are no signs of forced entry; it is quite another matter to exclude the presence of a second man because Lady Lucan saw no signs of a second man. The fact that Lady Lucan did not see another man does not mean that one was not there.

The presumption of innocence, a basic axiom of the common law, is not a literal presumption; except in a limited, technical sense, it is mythical. 'The accused is presumed to be innocent until proven guilty'; if this were literally true, then the accused would never be accused. Nobody goes around accusing people presumed to be innocent; that sort of behaviour is rightly considered to be a public nuisance.

There is, however, one form of behaviour which, in the general opinion, leads to a literal presumption of guilt, and that is to flee from the scene of the crime. In the popular mind that simple fact is probably the most compelling piece of evidence against Lord Lucan. There are, in addition, other compelling points to be made against him on the basis of the evidence established so far.

The first is that there was no sign that any struggle had taken place in any part of the basement which could be seen from the pavement. Lucan's stated motive for entering the house is, therefore, unexplained.

The second is that the police, in a test which could have been repeated by the defence, were unable to see what he claimed he could see from the pavement. His account would therefore, on this point, seem to be untrue.

The third is that a piece of piping similar to the bludgeon, longer and heavier but also wrapped in tape and apparently cut by the same hacksaw blade, was found in the boot of the abandoned Ford Corsair which had been lent to Lucan.

The fourth is that blood stains in this car were either of the relevant groups, A and B, or of AB, that is, either a third group or a mixture of the other two.

The fifth is that grey-blue wool fibres, which were microscopically indistinguishable from each other, were found on the bludgeon, in the basement, on a bath towel, in a wash-basin and in the car. No fibres were found on the mailbag. The fibres had 'almost certainly' been left by the same person. Someone therefore touched the bludgeon, entered the basement, used a bath towel and a wash-basin at 46 Lower Belgrave Street and entered the Ford Corsair. But that person did not touch the mailbag. Lord Lucan was wearing grey flannel trousers with blood stains on them, according to his friend Mrs Maxwell-Scott. He would therefore need to explain why he had touched the murder weapon, leaving no fingerprints. But the police would need to consider why no fibres were found on the mailbag. If a man is scattering wool fibres on everything he touches, why does he leave none on a bag into which he is forcing a doubled-up body? Lord Lucan would also need to explain why a twin bludgeon was found in the car he was driving. It can reasonably be assumed that he drove to Uckfield in the Ford Corsair, since he drove to Uckfield and since his own Mercedes was found parked outside his flat in Elizabeth Street without any trace of blood stains.

There is no point in pretending that the case against Lord Lucan is not very serious. None the less, on the evidence published so far, I think it unlikely that he murdered Sandra

Rivett. In fact, in my opinion, it is quite impossible for him to have done so. And there is an element of sentiment in the evidence that gets him off. Even had Lucan wished to deny that he had been inside No. 46 on the night of the murder, he could not have done so because his daughter, Frances, saw him there. It was her unforeseeable glimpse of him that would appear to have destroyed for him any chance of an alibi defence. The sentiment lies in the fact that it is also Frances's evidence which clears him of murder. He *did* have an alibi. In establishing this alibi and timing his movements and Mrs Rivett's death, there are five separate timetables to be reconciled.

The first is provided by the staff of the Clermont Club. The deputy manager said that Lord Lucan booked a table over the telephone 'at about 8.30'. The Club's linkman said that he had a conversation with Lord Lucan, at the door of the Club, 'about fifteen minutes later'. We can therefore take it that Lucan drove away from the Clermont Club in his Mercedes at about 8.45. This car was found parked outside his basement flat in Elizabeth Street. There were no signs of blood in it. We can therefore conclude that Lucan did not enter the Mercedes after he left Lower Belgrave Street, and we can assume that he parked it outside his flat before he entered his wife's house. It takes *at least* five minutes to drive through light traffic from the Clermont Club to Elizabeth Street. (In my own attempts I have never done it in less than seven minutes.) It takes *at least* five minutes to walk from Elizabeth Street to 46 Lower Belgrave Street and, in order to kill Mrs Rivett, he would then have had to enter the house, remove the light bulb in the 'basement' and conceal himself. Of course, he could have run from one house to the other, but we are dealing, on the suggestion of the police, with a man who was plotting a cold-blooded murder. Anyone 6 foot 4 inches in height running through Belgravia at 8.50 on a November night would have attracted attention. If he had dressed as a jogger, in Belgravia he would have begun to look like Burglar Bill. Therefore Lucan could not possibly have been in the basement of No. 46 before 8.55, even if everything had gone completely smoothly, and 9.00 would be a far more likely time.

His wife, according to the police, was in the habit of making a cup of tea 'at approximately 9.00'. Anyone intending to attack her, and being reasonably prudent about his plan, would therefore have been in the house by 8.40; 8.30 would have been a safer time. Lucan would hardly have been outside the Clermont Club at 8.45 if he intended to bash his wife on the head in the basement of Lower Belgrave Street, having first removed the light bulb, at 'approximately 9.00'.

The second timetable is provided by Veronica Lucan. She compiled it over the course of several days in the statement she made to the police in St George's Hospital while she was recovering from an attack that nearly ended her life. It is reasonable to suppose that in the crucial, vivid details of her ordeal she would be reliable but in the unimportant background matters she might be less precise.

She said that Sandra had offered to go down to make tea at 8.55 and that she followed Sandra down into the darkened house at about 9.15. She then described a brief fight. She had a glass of water in the cloakroom. Her husband helped her upstairs. They had a brief conversation in the bedroom and she ran out of the house. She gave the time of her exit as 9.59. Even by her own account, forty-four minutes were filled by two brief conversations and a short fight. In the state she was in, she could hardly be expected to notice the time. And the calmer minds in the Plumber's Arms gave a less surprising time for her dramatic entry – 9.45. So, as one might expect, she seems to have been slightly inaccurate when asked to estimate the time.

The third timetable is provided by Frances Bingham. One can expect the evidence of a 10-year-old child to be truthful but somewhat vague, particularly on the matter of time. But Frances did not *estimate* the time; she obtained it by reference to a crucial part of the life of a 10-year-old child on the way to bed – television programmes. Her statement was punctuated by the world of the small screen. It started at teatime. Tea was taken in the nursery with her mother, Sandra, her sister Camilla and her brother George 'at about 3.30 p.m.'.

After tea I played one of my games in the nursery. At 7.20 I watched *Top of the Pops* on TV in the nursery. Mummy, Camilla, George and Sandra were downstairs watching *The Six Million Dollar Man*. I joined them at 8.05 and we all watched TV in Mummy's room. When the programme finished at 8.30 I went back to the nursery and played with my game. Sandra brought Camilla and George upstairs and put them to bed. I had had my bath and was wearing my pyjamas. I stayed in the nursery about five minutes. I went downstairs again to Mummy's room at about 8.40. I asked Mummy where Sandra was and Mummy said she was downstairs making tea.

After a while Mummy said she wondered why Sandra was so long. It was before the *News* came on at 9 p.m. I said I would go downstairs to see what was keeping her, but Mummy said, no, she would go down. She left the bedroom door open, but there was no light in the hall. Just after Mummy left the room I heard a scream. It sounded as though it came from a long way away. I thought perhaps the cat had scratched Mummy and she had screamed. I was not frightened. I went to the door and called Mummy but there was no answer and I left it.

At 9.05 the *News* was on TV and Daddy and Mummy both walked into the room. Mummy had blood over her face and was crying. Mummy told me to go upstairs. Daddy didn't say anything to me and I said nothing to either of them. I don't know how much blood was on her face. I didn't hear any conversation between Mummy and

Daddy. I didn't see any blood on Daddy's clothes. I
wondered what had happened but I didn't ask.

She added that she went upstairs, went to bed and read a
book. Later she heard her father call out, 'Veronica, where
are you?' She went outside, looked over the banister and saw
her father walking out of the bedroom and into the bathroom
on the floor below. Then he went downstairs. 'That was the
last I saw of him. He never came up to the top of the house
either to look for Mummy or to say goodnight to me.'

As far as timings go, this is a devastating catalogue for
the police to deal with. 'I watched *Top of the Pops* . . . Mummy,
Camilla, George and Sandra were downstairs watching *The
Six Million Dollar Man*': this has the authentic ring of ob-
servation. 'I joined them at 8.05.' She can remember the
afternoon and evening because of the two television sets.
'When the programme finished at 8.30 . . .' Frances, aged
10, was not to know that commercial television programmes,
with the exception of the *News*, do not finish and start at the
advertised times. They finish a little early and start a little
late so that, at the advertised times, everyone is crowded
round the screen watching the advertisements. She and Camilla and George and Sandra would have gone upstairs a little
before 8.30. Sandra put Camilla and George to bed and then
disappeared. Frances continued to play her game for 'about
five minutes'. She estimates that when she returned to her
mother's room it was 'about 8.40'. It was almost certainly a
little later, but by that time Sandra had already set out for
the kitchen. Time passed. Her mother began to wonder where
Sandra was. Her mother stated that twenty minutes elapsed
between Sandra's setting out and her own departure to find
out what she was doing. Frances says, quite definitely, 'It
was before the *News* came on at 9 p.m.' That is persuasive.
Not many people set out to make tea when the news headlines
are imminent. You want to be settled, with your tea, as the

programme starts. Lady Lucan probably went downstairs at about 8.57. Sandra had probably set out about fifteen to twenty minutes earlier, say between 8.37 and 8.42, as Frances suggested.

The Home Office pathologist, Dr Keith Simpson, found that Mrs Rivett's death had been caused by suffocation. There had been considerable internal bleeding from her skull injuries into her throat. Because she was unconscious she would have been unable to clear her air passages by coughing, and she would have died within a minute or two, before her body was placed in the sack. By 8.45, when Lord Lucan was talking to the linkman at the door of the Clermont Club, Sandra Rivett was almost certainly dead.

To summarize, the points against the police case that Lord Lucan attempted to murder his wife are the following.

Lucan had no motive to behave in the way described. The motive ascribed to him by the police is that he was a professional gambler, on a losing streak, getting deeper and deeper into debt, who could no longer afford to maintain his wife and children at the house in Lower Belgrave Street and who therefore decided on this course of action. Against that it must be said that he had no chance of concealing his wife's body, or the manner of her death, by killing her in the way that Mrs Rivett was killed.

An alternative motive is that he wished to recover his children. Again he would have had no chance of recovering his children by being found to have murdered their mother. He would have been imprisoned, without his children, for a considerable period, and on his release he might have found that their affection for the man who had killed their mother was to some extent blighted.

A third motive, which has in the past been put forward by Lady Lucan, was that he simply wished to recover the house, as it was by far his most valuable possession and he planned to sell it to pay off his debts and fund his gambling. He knew that he could not sell the house so long as she continued to live there. Apart from the fact that he did not own the lease to the house, this runs into the same objection as the other two motives. You don't need the value of a house in Belgravia to stake your gambling in Parkhurst Prison. The ferocity with which Sandra Rivett was struck would seem to be contrary to any motive Lucan might have had.

There is, of course, the possible explanation that in striking in the dark the woman whom he believed to be his wife he simply lost control of himself. That cannot be ruled out, but it remains unlikely. A man who had worked out an elaborate plan, even going to the extent of bandaging the murder weapons and providing himself with an alibi that required him to appear in public in a fashionable club at 8.45 and 11 p.m., would seem to have been committed to a state of mind in which he could afford no slips. If he was going to do the thing, he had to do it exactly. There must be no trace of his wife's death in the house, and there must be no sign of his recent act about him when he walked into the Clermont Club.

There are two further reasons why it seems to me unlikely that Lord Lucan behaved in the way the police have suggested. The first is that, given the police motive, there was a serious disadvantage in launching a solo attack on his wife. If he did that, how could he ensure that the scene was not observed by one of his children? Particularly if a scream was heard, one of his children might well have followed their mother downstairs. It would have been as important for Lucan to conceal the truth from his children as it was to conceal the truth from the police.

The second reason is that he would never have chosen to kill his wife with a bludgeon. As we have seen, the disadvantages of a bludgeon attack in the dark were all too predictable. One might well start off thinking that one was just going to bash someone on the head, knock her out and then kill her some other way. But as soon as the details began to present themselves this method of attack would have ruled itself out. Two of John Lucan's friends, who knew him for some time, both before he got married and subsequently, have told me that the one aspect of the story they find impossible to accept is the use of a bludgeon. Even if he had decided to kill his wife, they say, they cannot believe that he would have done it in such a brutal and violent manner.

Is John Lucan, therefore, innocent? Can we, to start with, accept his explanation that he was just passing the house by chance, saw through the windows a fight taking place and entered in order to intervene? The police have discredited that story. But if he knew what had happened at No. 46 that night, why did he give such an unbelievable account of his own presence? The answer is that Lucan has not given a true account of why he entered the house that night for a reason that is in itself to his credit. He failed to give a convincing reason for his presence in the house *because he did not know that no struggle had taken place in the front basement*. He did not know because he was not there. None the less he gave a false account of his true reasons for being in the house. So what was he trying to conceal? And what did he know?

Lucan is known to have been preoccupied with his children. His mother and several of his friends described him as 'abnormally' concerned with the children's welfare; it had become an obsession. Not every father can accept the right of a court to deprive him of the company of his children. Young children are, as a rule, placed in the care of their mother. If the father considers that the mother is unfit to look after them, he loses all faith in the courts and in the legal system which has placed his children at hazard, and he sees himself as their only protection. He is driven to act. But people who act against the decisions of the courts become outlaws. They are a threat to social order. They attract attention from social agencies. If they are regarded as *disturbed*, they fall into the hands of social workers. If they are regarded as *rational*, they become the concern of the police. There was nothing more that Lucan could do to rescue his children except risk putting himself in this impossible position. He had reached that point in a custody battle where a fashionable lawyer advises his wealthy client that his only remaining recourse is to place both himself and his children beyond the reach of the courts, out of their jurisdiction. Abroad.

Most men in Lucan's position might have taken that advice. Plenty of separated fathers and mothers have taken it in the past. But it was not very suitable advice for Lucan. He seems to have been a man of very limited independent resources. He was a creature of habit ('smoked salmon, lamb cutlets, smoked salmon . . .'); without any doubt, in W. S. Gilbert's sense, he was an *English* man. He wanted his children to lead, in so far as it was possible, an *English* life. One could just about make out a case for Lucan's explanation of 'a night of unbelievable coincidence', of a sequence of events in which he entered the house as part of a carefully conceived plan to remove his children from the custody of their mother, believing it to be the nanny's night off, and found he had chosen a night when the nanny was not after all off and some total stranger, better informed than he, had entered the house in order to beat the nanny to death. One could go along with a story like that – his presence in the house explained, the bloodstains on his clothing explained, the fibres on the bludgeon explained by the fact that he, in horror, picked it up, the bloodstains in the car explained – except for one thing: the police evidence that in the boot of the car lay a twin bludgeon, also bandaged. Nothing can explain why, if Lucan was intent on the ferocious action of snatching his children, and Mr X was intent on the ferocious action of murdering Mrs Rivett, Lucan should end up with half of this total stranger's murder weapon in the boot of his borrowed car.

So we have a situation in which Lucan did not kill Sandra

Rivett because he was elsewhere, but she was murdered by someone wielding a weapon whose twin lay in the boot of Lucan's car. How can these two notions be reconciled? The solution, I suggest, is as follows.

Lucan wanted to recover custody of his children and continue to live in England. Having exhausted his legal remedies, he was driven to extra-legal action: crime. Having concluded that his wife was mad, unfit to look after his children, implacable and a more plausible witness than he, he decided that she would have to die. He did not, however, wish to kill her himself: 'The shadow on the ceiling will not be mine, my darling . . .' So he arranged for an accomplice.

His plan was this. Lucan borrowed Michael Stoop's Ford Corsair, a nondescript car with a capacious boot. He purchased a speedboat and moved it up the coast from Chichester to Newhaven. He undertook a course of physical training to prepare himself for the task ahead. He then recruited his partner. On the night of the murder he let this man into the house, having previously provided him with instructions as to where he could conceal himself. Then he departed to give himself an alibi.

At about 8.30 the children would be sent to bed. He knew their timetable because he was very well informed about their daily routine; he questioned both them and the latest nanny regularly. All the children would already have had their bath and would be on the second floor, watching television. Between 8.30 and 9.00 the two smaller children would be put to bed; Frances would get ready for bed; Veronica would go to the kitchen and make herself a cup of tea; Veronica and Frances would then together watch the *Nine O'Clock News*. That was the predictable routine.

Lucan, therefore, would have driven the Mercedes to a point near the mews and, using his Yale key, let himself into No. 46, through the front door, at about 8.15. He would have checked that everyone was upstairs, removed the light bulb from the basement, and waited for the shadowy figure who was his accomplice to emerge from the November night. This man would have been told that he would have to wait in the basement for fifteen or twenty minutes for his victim to descend. Once the killer was inside, Lucan would have telephoned the Clermont Club at about 8.30 to book a table for four. (He could have made this call from his cottage in the mews which backed onto Lower Belgrave Street and which was cut off from No. 46 by the high wall enclosing the back yard. He had leased this cottage to Greville Howard but Howard was at the theatre that evening.) Then Lucan would have taken the Mercedes and driven to the Clermont Club, appearing there at 8.45, so giving himself, as he thought, an alibi. He would then have driven quickly back to his own flat, parked the Mercedes, switched to the Ford and returned to Lower Belgrave Street, he would have parked out of sight of No. 46 and let himself into the house at about 9.00. We can assume he had a torch. He would have realized immediately that something was wrong. There would have been blood all over the basement, a mailbag leaking blood and the sounds of a struggle.

As he approached the stairs to the hall his accomplice would have heard him or seen his torchlight and fled, possibly through the back door into the enclosed back yard.* At this point Veronica, freed from the struggle, would have screamed, and she would have heard her husband's voice, in the dark, telling her to 'shut up'. In an attempt to keep her quiet, desperate that the children should not discover what was going on, he would have thrust his hand over and then into her mouth. Shortly after that she attached herself to his

---

* This would explain how blood came to be found on leaves in the back yard, a fact which is inexplicable if one accepts the police version of events. Lucan would have known that there was no exit through the back door. But a blood-stained hitman, fleeing through the back door in a panic, could have turned back by the high wall before finding his way out through the front door.

testicles, he removed his hand from her throat and they both calmed down. The question of Sandra's disappearance would have been raised; he would then have realized what had happened and that his plans were hopelessly upset. The game was apparently up.

They would have gone upstairs before 9.30 to attend to her wounds, both of them needing time to think. She then seized the first opportunity to run from the house. As Frances noted in her statement, Lucan called out, 'Veronica, where are you?' He then disappeared downstairs and 'never came up to the top of the house' to look for Veronica. The reason must be that when he went down to the front door he looked down the street, saw his wife running along the pavement towards the pub and realized that the last string was broken. He could no longer control what his wife was going to say; he had only a minute or so to get out of the house before she raised the alarm. It was about 9.45. He would have picked up the spare bludgeon, but he would not have touched the mailbag. If he had left the Ford in a position that was convenient for the mews, he would himself have left by the front door and set off in the opposite direction to the Plumber's Arms. He would have shut the front door behind him, mindful of the children and anxious also to delay the pursuit. He then went to an unknown address and telephoned Mrs Floorman, having first failed to get her to answer her doorbell. His motive for talking to Mrs Floorman would have been to ask her, because she was close, to go to No. 46, since the children were now alone in the house with a corpse in the basement. But he was too shocked to hold the conversation, so he paused for some time and then, still shocked, telephoned his mother. This call did not come from a call-box. It would have been about 10.25. His mother arrived at the house at 10.45 to find that the police had broken the door in at about 10.05 and that the CID had arrived at 10.20.

———

Had things gone according to plan, Lucan would have transferred the US mailbag containing his wife's body into the large safe that stood in the basement. He would have cleared up the few signs of a struggle that he anticipated finding, and left by the front door. He would then, presumably, have completed his alibi by going to the house to which he eventually went to telephone his mother. Whoever was at that house would have sworn, under oath, that he had arrived shortly after 8.45.

Lucan would then have arranged for someone to telephone No. 46 and ask to speak to Veronica. On being told by Frances that she could not be found and that it was Sandra's night out, that person would have gone round there to be with the children and would have left a message for Lucan at the Clermont. Perhaps that is why Lucan booked a table for four rather than five, because he knew that as soon as he arrived at the Clermont, between 10.30 and 11.00, he would find a message for him to go to No. 46. He would have waited at No. 46 until Sandra's return, checking the safe and probably taking the opportunity to remove, surreptitiously, Veronica's handbag and an overcoat. On the following day, a Friday, he would normally have picked the children up at 5.30 anyway. On this occasion he would have given Sandra the weekend off and, towards the end of the day, reported that his wife had been missing for nearly twenty-four hours. The police would have taken very little notice of this routine report until the Monday morning.

On either the Thursday or the Friday night Lucan would have returned to the house, let himself in, transferred his wife's body from the safe to the boot of the Corsair, driven to Newhaven, motored his boat out into the waters above Seven-Mile Bottom and disposed of the weighted sack. By the time Sandra returned from her weekend off on Sunday evening to pick up the children at 5.30, the house would have been ready for inspection. When the police began to take an interest on Monday morning, doubtless in response to Lucan's anxious inquiries, Veronica would have been dead and gone for more than three days. All the police would have had to go on was that a solitary woman, with a history of mental disturbance, who had once disappeared in the centre of London for several hours, had left her house one evening, taking with her a handbag and coat, never to be seen again.

It may be wondered why, if the manner in which Sandra Rivett was killed is an objection to Lucan's doing the job, it should not be an objection to someone else's doing it. Who, after all, was the accomplice? Here Lucan would have had a choice between someone he knew and someone he didn't. The advantage of a friend would have been that he was trustworthy. But it is one thing to ask a trusted friend to assist you in a murder plot in which you play the murderer. It is quite another to ask the friend to do the murder for you. That would be pushing friendship rather far. It is much more likely that Lucan hired a hitman, just as Veronica feared he would. That is why he borrowed £3,000, at an exorbitant rate of interest, a few weeks before the murder. That would have been about the going rate. And there is one great advantage to hiring a hitman. Provided you use an intermediary, you never meet each other. The hitman need never know whom he is killing, and you never know who did the job. The hitman would have been given a plan of the ground floor and basement, told there would be no light, given a timetable, told that his victim would be a slightly built woman, told that there would be a sack in the basement into which he should put the body and told not to make a mess or a disturbance. Since Lady Lucan's disappearance would probably never have led to a murder inquiry, he might well never have realized whom he had killed. So what went wrong? The answer must be pure speculation, but here is one set of facts which would fit.

The hitman would have been paid half in advance and half

in arrears. Three thousánd pounds would have purchased the services of a reliable specialist. On the night in question the specialist was at the last moment indisposed. Maybe he sprained his wrist; maybe he was under arrest for some previous engagement. But, loath to lose the remaining £1,500, he sent a deputy. This man, obtained quickly, was not a specialist. He was clumsy and he lacked the 'bottle'. He therefore drank too much before starting work. Finally, he could not even decide what length of cosh to use. So he cobbled up two.* Instead of making a neat, quick job of it, he made a dreadful mess. Twenty minutes after his initial attack, still drunkenly struggling to get his victim's body into the bag, he heard another woman descending the stairs, calling, 'Sandra, Sandra.' He thereupon panicked and attacked her as well. But he was unfit, drunk and frightened, and now, in the hallway, on unfamiliar ground in a darkened house; furthermore, his bludgeon, seriously distorted by the first attack, was no longer an efficient club. Veronica Lucan was therefore able to survive the second attack. This was the fight which Lucan, arriving to clear up, interrupted.

Lucan then, in his own shock and dismay, made two mistakes over the bludgeons. He picked up the murder weapon, perhaps intending to remove it. He threw it into the cloakroom lest one of the children should come as far as the hall and see it. On descending to look for Veronica, and realizing that she had escaped into the street, he forgot all about the murder weapon in his own haste to get away. But on his way out he picked up the second bludgeon, the clean one, and removed it from the scene of the crime. Having pocketed the

---

* The murder weapon was between 8 and 10 inches long and weighed 2¼ pounds. The second piece of piping was 16½ inches long. The standard Metropolitan Police truncheon is 16 inches long. The new baton ordered for riot control is 28 inches long, although Lieutenant-Colonel W. E. Fairbairn, formerly Deputy Commissioner, the Shanghai Municipal Police Force, and one-time adviser on riot techniques to the Colonial Office, after a lifetime of scholarship, swore by the length of 20 inches.

spare weapon, Lucan would later have transferred it to the boot of the Ford and forgotten about it. As the night wore on he drank whisky and vodka, and took four Valium. Forgetting the bludgeon in the boot was to be his last mistake of the night, and his most serious one. Without the twin bludgeon in the boot, none of the evidence, forensic or from witnesses, would have been enough in itself to contradict his story that he surprised a stranger.

There is another, entirely separate, reason to believe that Lucan had an accomplice. In his letter to Bill Shand Kydd he wrote: 'For George and Frances to go through life knowing their father had been in the dock accused of attempted murder would be too much for them.' It is significant that he wrote 'accused of attempted murder', not 'accused of murder'. Lucan never believed that he would be accused of murder because he had not murdered Sandra Rivett; he had an alibi for the time when she was murdered, and he could not foresee that there would be a discrepancy between the timetables given by Veronica and Frances, and that Veronica's would be preferred. He did, however, foresee that he would be accused of what Veronica was convinced he had done – attempt to murder her. As he wrote to Shand Kydd: 'V. accused me of having hired him.' This is persuasive additional evidence for the accomplice theory.

Of course, the accomplished theory leaves one further question unsolved. If Lord Lucan did not do it, who did kill Sandra Rivett? Somewhere in England an inexperienced contract killer, who botched a brutal murder, is walking free. Whoever he is, he has left behind him a most remarkable trail of havoc.

Many people are convinced that Lord Lucan is dead because his body has never been found. I do not agree with that deduction. If he had sunk his speedboat in a deep part of the Channel, having first chained himself to it, his body would still be at the bottom of the sea. The *Mary Rose*, a Tudor warship that sank in the Solent and was recently refloated, still contained the skeletons of many Tudor sailors. Alternatively, Lord Lucan could have killed himself in some other way, having arranged for one of his friends to dispose of his body.

But did he kill himself? In the first place, he was a gambler. Gamblers believe in luck. Suicide leaves you with no chances. In the gambling world it is taken for granted that Lucan is alive. Living in hiding is difficult and expensive. But Lucan, as his friends have testified, was not short of offers of help from rich friends. And if he was unjustly accused, he would have had a very strong motive to 'lie doggo' until the moment arrived when he could emerge to clear his name.

If one accepts the accomplice theory, then Lucan would be guilty of conspiracy to murder, an offence that carries the same penalty as the act itself. But would he now be convicted? His main hope of acquittal would lie in raising doubts about the prosecution's timetable and in attacking the credibility of his wife. Since November 1981 it has been possible for his wife or his heirs to apply for a writ of presumption of death. Such a writ would end the Lucans' marriage, which would mean that if Lucan were ever tried, Lady Lucan could give evidence against him in regard to the attack on Sandra Rivett. Until such a writ is granted Lord Lucan's son, Lord Bingham, cannot take his seat in the House of Lords, nor can Lord Lucan's will take effect and his property remains in the possession of his wife. But, for some reason, up till now no application has been made for the writ.

If Lucan were alive, what would he look like? Had Dominick Elwes allowed his imagination to dwell on this question, we would have seen Lord Lucan reduced to a height of 5 feet 10 inches, having visited in ex-Nazi orthopaedic surgeon practising in Guatemala with long experience of shortening the shin bones. His nose (perhaps hooked), his jaw (reduced), his eyes (altered in colour by contact lenses) – none would be recognizable. He would be managing an Argentinian beef ranch or overseeing some Central American oil camp. He would be speaking English but with a 'Canadian' accent. It is the sort of fantasy that Elwes would have made utterly convincing. But it remains a fantasy.

Unlike some of his fellow gamblers, John Lucan was the genuine 'Crimean' article. The Earl of Raglan, who held the ultimate responsibility for the débâcle of Balaclava, died on the shores of the Black Sea in 1855 of a broken heart. He said that he could never return to England 'because they would stone me to death'. There is, of course, no real comparison to be made between Lord Raglan in 1855 and Lord Lucan in 1974. The only real similarity is that John Lucan tried to model his own behaviour on nineteenth-century standards of honour. It was this unreal approach to life that led to the tragic events of that night, and by the end of the débâcle of Belgravia there was only one honourable solution. Reading the two letters that Lucan wrote to his friends on the night of 7–8 November, one can detect a hardening of purpose. There is no mention in the second letter, to Michael Stoop, of 'lying doggo for a while'. There is only a repeated concern for his children and a last message to them. One can therefore conclude that Lord Lucan also decided against being 'stoned to death' and took the necessary steps to ensure that he was never tried, either for the murder he did not commit or for the conspiracy he did.

Index